BUT WITH THE DAWN, REJOICING

I will extol you, O LORD, for you drew me clear and did not let my enemies rejoice over me.

O LORD, my God, I cried out to you and you healed me.

O LORD, you brought me up from the nether world; you preserved me from among those going down into the pit.

Sing praise to the LORD, you his faithful ones, and give thanks to his holy name.

For his anger lasts but a moment; a lifetime, his good will.

At nightfall, weeping enters in, but with the dawn, rejoicing.

Psalm 29 (30):2–6

Mary Ellen Kelly

BUT WITH THE DAWN, REJOICING

The Bruce Publishing Company • Milwaukee

With Ecclesiastical Permission

Library of Congress Catalog Card Number: 59–10531

(Second Printing — 1960)

This book is lovingly dedicated to

MY MOTHER

without whom I could not have written one paragraph. To her, and to my heavenly Mother, I am eternally and inexpressibly grateful.

ACKNOWLEDGMENTS

To Rev. Peter Fiolek, C.R., editor of *The Banner*, 1445 W. Division St., Chicago, Ill., for permission to use two of my columns as the basis of my last chapter.

To Rev. Roger M. Charest, S.M.M., editor of *Queen of All Hearts*, Bay Shore, L. I., N. Y., for making me more aware of our Lady, for insisting on the best articles I could submit, for continued encouragement, constructive criticism, and enormous kindness.

To Lenora Mattingly Weber, friend and writer, for spare-nothing, phrase-by-phrase analysis of each chapter, and for considering me a writer first and an invalid second.

To Rev. Leo P. McCoy, my pastor, for guiding me through rewrites, dangling participles, rejections, and all difficult spellings.

To Professor Walter S. Campbell (in memoriam), the University of Oklahoma Journalism director who, through two correspondence courses and 13 following years, gave me instruction far beyond the call of duty. During this time I always regretted our not having met; now I regret his not seeing my book in print. But maybe in the blessedness that is heaven, both he and my father will get a glimpse of BUT WITH THE DAWN, REJOICING.

CONTENTS

PART 1

CHAPTER 1

MOMENT OF DECISION

DATE: *November 16, 1939*
PLACE: *St. Joseph's Mercy Hospital*
Sioux City, Iowa
TIME: *To Blow Out the Candles*

It was my seventeenth birthday. For years I had dreamed of this milestone when I would be a senior, wear high heels, and stay out late. Now the day had come, and I had never felt less like celebrating. I was seventeen, but my school days were over. Instead of wearing heels I had on bedroom slippers, and as for staying out late, right then my only desire was to be lifted back into bed.

My hospital room looked festive. Birthday cards covered the dresser, four guests graced the chairs, and frosted cake and ice cream extended the theme of a happy celebration. My visitors kept reassuring me that I'd soon be up and out, but I was not so sure. Of course I didn't let on, because this was part of the strange subterfuge carried on between the sick and the healthy. Miserable and cramped in a high-backed wooden rocker, I prayed for the party to end.

A month before I had come to the hospital in such acute pain from rheumatoid arthritis that all I wanted was relief. I tried any medication eagerly, hoping for some magic pill or "shot" to lessen the agony of my joints.

Slowly and with seeming malice, October had dragged by. When November took over, the leaves and days began to vanish alternately in the autumn whirlwind. I began to think about Christmas and it became my number one thought. I dreamed of Mother's turkey—of my brother, Robert, decorating our tree—of Dad—of friends and good things to smell, and of my white cat, Sir Galahad, with a big red ribbon around his neck. Each moment of dreaming made me more determined to be home for Christmas.

To insure against a sudden loss of speech (my doctor always scared me so I usually forgot what I intended to ask) I had rehearsed several approaches. Surely one of them would stand by me. It wasn't likely for him to give an answer while others were present. So I had more reasons than pain and tiredness for wanting the party to end.

At last, on a bleak December morning, the right moment presented itself when the doctor walked into my room. A thousand needles jabbed into my hands and the soles of my feet. A trickle of perspiration wandered down my spine.

I managed somehow to conceal my panic and frame my question. Then I silently watched the surgeon walk toward the window and stare out. He was so long answering that I wondered if he had heard me. Finally, his glance still fixed on something beyond the window, he said rather gruffly, "Sorry kid, not for Christmas." Without glancing back, he turned and left the room.

The first few times I returned the greeting, "Merry Christmas, Kelly," it stuck in my throat. But as the day neared, the hospital became less impersonal. Friends decorated my room with a small tree and a cardboard crib depicting the nativity. Nurses and doctors tossed in cheery greetings, unknown passersby murmured well-meant platitudes, and Johnny, the paper boy (now a priest), left me a free Sioux City *Journal* every morning. To reject the warmth offered was like being in my mother's kitchen while she is baking, and refusing a hot biscuit.

Then quickly, Christmas came. Just as quickly it departed, leaving me with a generous supply of bath powder, bed jackets, and African violets. When the day's events ended and the hospital noises blended with faint strains of "Silent Night," I thanked the Infant Christ for being good to me, and once again wished Him a happy birthday.

As darkness closed around me, I admitted for the first time that I was a helpless invalid. My jaws were locked; spine, hips, knees, and ankles were rigid; elbows, wrists, fingers were poker-stiff. My shoulders were about two per cent less unyielding. I was surprised that so few tears accompanied this admission, but in ten weeks I had learned that crying made things worse for me. Why? Because I couldn't brush the tears away, and when they rolled into my ears, they tickled like flies.

When, I wondered, did I first see it coming? There in the darkness, I looked back for signposts. The first one I could distinguish was a cigar box which contains thirteen long brown curls. You might say that with this box my story begins in a tree-shaded Iowa town called Marcus.

CHAPTER 2

WHERE TALL CORN (AND LITTLE GIRLS) GROW

"GOODNESS knows Mary Ellen is active enough," my mother explained to our doctor. "She stands on her head, turns somersaults, hangs by her knees from trees. And yet, her knees swell and get stiff, so something, somewhere, is wrong. . . ."

Something was wrong, all right, but the doctors seemed unable to pinpoint it. "Maybe she's growing too fast. See that she rests more."

So I rested. A year later my parents took a layman's advice: "Cut her hair! It's sapping her strength!" Off went my curls, which were stored away in a cigar box. For the next three years I saw no reason for the concern over my health. I seldom missed a day at Holy Name School, played ball, roller-skated, searched for green apples and rhubarb. Then came another signpost.

"Can't you straighten your arms any farther than that?" a friend asked. The answer was no. "Can't you sit on your heels, either?" A brief experiment showed I couldn't. I also noticed that my right foot was different, a discovery I revealed only to my mother.

"Don't worry, darling," she said. "With God's help, your arms and feet will straighten and be strong again soon."

A year later my vanity as well as my curiosity was aroused when a swollen knuckle received the splint-and-bandage treatment. My classmates questioned me about my obvious plight, and never was a battle wound treated with more respect.

This childish pride lost its appeal with the advent of my twelfth winter, for with it came pain which was more or less to be my companion the remainder of my life. It tagged along wherever I went, interferred with nearly everything I did, and interrupted my sleep.

It was 1935. A golden-haired moppet named Shirley Temple made another smash movie, and my favorite actor, Lew Ayres, married Ginger Rogers. To a poor French-Canadian couple five daughters had been recently born, and in a tragic plane crash Will Rogers and Wiley Post lost their lives.

In Marcus, my life also took a new turn when Mother closed the candy and coffee shop she had operated on Main Street since 1932. Lifesaver it had been, but a grueling responsibility. We fought heat in summer, cold in winter, and struggled the year-round to remember that the customer is always right. The novelty of being on Main Street appealed strongly for a while, but wore off when the Depression withdrew all the usual reasons for going downtown after supper. The room behind our shop was dreary on winter evenings, and the nuisance of a pot-bellied stove and outdoor plumbing didn't add to the attraction.

Most tiresome of all was the nightly exodus to our home, a block away. With a loyal but foolhardy poodle named Officer Pat leading the homeward trek, the Kellys trudged along, no richer than they had been that morning but grateful to the Eternal Provider for having fed, clothed, and sheltered us one more day.

But that was over now, and Mother and I loved being home all day again. She roamed about like a tourist, examined her neglected geraniums, picked lilies of the valley and lilacs for bouquets, and looked with pride at her wash-filled clotheslines. Things took a better turn for Dad too, who was 57, and had been working as a W.P.A. timekeeper. For nearly twenty years he had owned his own business and given his family everything they wanted. Then, after 1929, everything changed. He didn't complain or lose patience, yet the sparkle in his eyes had dimmed, and gone from his voice was that special lilt that seems to be inherent in people born in Ireland's County Mayo. Now with a job in the offing, a hint of his former zest returned.

"We will say a novena for your brother Robert," Mother announced, "that he will get a good job." For boys of 17, that meant a near miracle in the Mid-Thirty's. Confident that our prayers were never wasted, we persisted whether our requests were answered or not. So for nine days we begged St. Jude, patron of difficult cases, to solve this problem. His promptness was noteworthy. On the tenth day Robert was summoned to clean a cistern.

On a bright June morning I kissed my folks good-by and set out with my aunt, Sister Mary Philomena, R.S.M., to see a well-known orthopedic surgeon in Sioux City. Perhaps Sister, a nurse, suspected what his diagnosis would be, but wisely she kept her counsel.

The examination was brief and painless. I dressed, then meekly ventured a question.

"Do you know what's wrong, Doctor?"

"Yes, my dear," the big man replied soberly. "You have rheumatoid arthritis."

After he left, I began writing a post card to Mom and Dad. Halfway through it, I hurried to the chart room and asked the nurse in charge how to spell those words Doctor had used.

They were not only hard to spell, they were hard to live with, too. Until school started, my address was St. Joseph Mercy Hospital, a fabulous combination of assembly line rehabilitation center, lost and found department, distillery of tears, and cradle of birth. Though not without their moments of loneliness and wondering, those weeks possessed an excitement that both stimulated and entertained me. Come to think of it, the word "taught" can also be used, for I had already begun to learn what a powerful equalizer is illness.

The passing of another year brought no improvement, but thanks to my folks and their faithful Essex, which I loved to drive, my eighth year of schooling was completed.

The following August the doctor operated on my right foot, removing the crippling calcium deposits along the metatarsal arch. This operation was my real introduction to pain — pain that ran like a wild and savage thing throughout my entire being.

But thanks to the resiliency of youth, pain subsided and the wounds healed. The surgery slowed me down, but not for long.

With crutches gripped firmly, an outsized shoe flopping on my bandaged foot, and Mother's "Be careful!" ringing in my ears, I entered Holy Name High School on a sweltering day in 1936.

To be "different" at fourteen is a dreadful thing, but to be different in a way that invokes sympathy is unbearable — at least for one with my pride. So I began a game of pretense that went on for years — all to avoid being the object of pity. One of my ruses was to keep one leg straight out under my desk in order to stand promptly when called on to recite, and in restaurants or sweet shops, I sat only on high stools.

I kept up this camouflage at home too. When stiffness in my knees made bending too painful, I used a hanger to pick up an article; or I would push it into a corner and then ease it up on to the chair with my crutches. While I could kick off my galoshes, I could not put them on alone, so I didn't wear them.

Arthritis or no, I still could dance. My excursions around the floor were confined to simple steps which required little knee-bending. Sometimes when I was more on the limber side, I ventured into the "Suzy-Q," the "Shuffle," and even did a little "Truckin'." I'm grateful for those dancing days, short though they were, and loved every minute spent in melodic escape from the stiffness and pain that tormented me when the music was no longer a distraction.

By mid-winter of my sophomore year, more and more effort was expended in laying a smoke screen to hide my increasing stiffness. When March came, I was so tired of pretending and of pain that I accepted my aunt's invitation to spend the rest of the winter with her in the Waverly, Iowa, hospital. Perhaps heat therapy might help. My days at Holy Name were concluded at a school dance. I laughed, sang, and danced the "Big Apple," 1938's popular mixer, with modifications. I'm glad I didn't know then that I would never be coming back to Holy Name. Good-bys were rough enough as it was.

In Sioux City, when I was twelve, pain had become my permanent house guest companion. Now in Waverly, three years later, loneliness moved in. As soon as street lights punctuated the darkness, I hurried to the unoccupied room across the hall from mine, perched on the window sill, and turned homesick eyes toward Marcus.

After Waverly I went to the Mayo Clinic in Rochester. For three days poker-stiff fingers probed and prodded me, X-ray machines stared through me, and for hours I paraded up and down draped in a long white sheet.

From all this searching we received this verdict: "Rheumatoid arthritis, and secondary anemia. All advisable treatment and medicines have been tried. Can suggest no further course."

As clearly as I can remember, my not entering school that fall in '39 was not a terrible tragedy; it was simply another demand made on me by the strange disease that was undeniably playing for keeps. But I never supposed that the struggle would go on indefinitely; I never supposed my school days were permanently ended.

As Dad was on the road almost every day and Mother cooked at a local restaurant, Sir Galahad, my loyal white cat, and I had both the house and the day to ourselves. After my routine duties were taken care of, I would stir up a batch of fudge or pop some corn and, with my cat curled up beside me, read for hours.

I crossed rivers with Halliburton; hunted with Osa and Martin Johnson on a Borneo safari; shivered through a Russian winter with Ludwig's Napoleon; eavesdropped while the Tudors bickered over affairs of state; cowered in the Bastille as the Paris of Dickens converged upon it in bloody pandemonium; wept with Jane Eyre when she discovered the awful truth. . . .

Then June promised a real adventure — a visit to Farley, Iowa, my mother's home town. Since plush predepression days when summer meant a cottage at nearby Lake Okoboji, my vacations had been spent in a hospital. This prospect consequently lifted my heart high up on a cloud.

The thud that came was not surprising; all hearts do the same when a cloud is suddenly pulled out from under one.

On the night of June 25 our family doctor rushed me to the hospital for an emergency appendectomy. When the anesthetic wore off, I thought of the pretty clothes that had been made for my trip. Only the seersucker housecoat was ever worn.

I repeatedly questioned the nun in charge about when I could go home. Why, she finally asked, was I in such a hurry to go home?

"Anyone would be eager, Sister, if his mother and dad made him feel as welcome as mine do."

My expectations were fully realized when I was brought home soon afterward. Mother served me a tray of fried chicken, potatoes, gravy as only she can make it, olives, celery, and fresh strawberries. Dad brought my bed downstairs so my convalescence would not be lonely, and neighbors and relatives came in to visit. Sir Galahad had disappeared shortly after I went to the hospital, but everything else was unchanged. I never wanted to leave home again.

The radio brought news, that fall of 1939, of purging and persecution in Poland and Czechoslovakia. The thought of the suffering of these people, made me forget my own distress for a while. But with each passing day my private war against arthritis took my strength until, even for the oppressed of Europe, I became too tired to cry.

My crutches, idle since my foot surgery four years earlier, kept me from being anchored when my knees became poker-stiff. This kind of automation was extremely painful but I welcomed any distraction, even such a strategic move as getting from the living room to the kitchen. The front porch was off limits: it had a threshold.

Then one morning one knee refused to straighten despite Mother's tender coaxing with hot rags. In less than a week the other knee followed suit; it simply would not release the cramped hold it had made during the night. So why cry? My fingers couldn't have grasped my crutches any longer anyway. The timing was perfect.

The nightmare of pain was now upon me in full production. Thank God my brother was at home at this time, for he relieved my position every two hours by scooping me up gently into his arms and placing me in a different chair. Musical chairs the hard way. He entertained me in grand style by playing the piano and singing songs we had shared and liked as we were growing up. His repertory wasn't large, but it was familiar.

At night Mother and Dad alternated their vigils, both of them turning me every two hours and one always within call. I still tried to conceal from them the growing urgency and desperation that came oftener now, but toward my brother there seemed to be less need of pretense. "You do think this will let up soon, don't you, Robert?" I soon stopped asking him that question however, because if there's anything that distresses me, it is to see a man cry.

On a blustery mid-October day I took another trip to St. Joseph's Hospital.

"Don't worry, dear," Mother whispered reassuringly before saying good-by. "You'll be home in a few weeks."

I remained at St. Joseph's for the next five years.

CHAPTER 3

NO STRANGER TO ME

THAT first Christmas in the hospital was the turning point in my life. I was an invalid. I had to accept that fact. The nurses, my family, and friends accepted it too. For by now my legs were drawn into a 45-degree angle, my fingers were too stiff to bend and my spine, wrists, and hips were almost rigid. Pain beat a dirge day and night, and my sixty-five pounds failed to cushion my bones where cushioning was needed. I had no more need to pretend. It didn't seem strange to me that I was bedfast. Hadn't the signposts all through my arthritic childhood pointed this way? Up until now I had been concerned only with one day, or perhaps an hour, at a time. But now, with a crippled future ahead, I knew I must plan my life accordingly. But before I had done much planning my doctor stopped at my bedside one day.

"Mary (he never called me by both names), how about another operation?"

"What am I to get rid of this time?"

He laughed. "Only the pressure on your bottom. If we don't straighten your legs, that thin tail bone of yours is likely to develop some bad bedsores. You wouldn't want that. It'll be a little rough at first but will prevent much future distress. Think about it, and I'll see you tomorrow."

The complete trust I had in this man left no room for qualms. I said yes.

The adhesions were broken and plaster casts applied from my hips to toes. Four years earlier the torture of my first surgery had found some release in the restless movements of my arms. Now I could only lie there while pain chewed on my bones.

Six weeks later the casts were removed. I waited for my doctor's verdict. "I hate to tell you this, Mary, but your legs have to be still straighter. We'll have to go through this once more." Then, as if trying to soften his announcement, he added: "This trip won't be nearly as bad, kid."

I looked at him fearfully. "You're sure?"

He nodded.

"My legs don't have to be like Marlene Dietrich's you know," I said hopefully.

Giving my knee a tender pat, the man I so admired and feared walked toward the door, then called back over his shoulder: "We'll settle for nothing less than Dietrich's."

Once again the adhesions in my knees were broken and casts applied. As my doctor promised, the post-surgery period wasn't so bad. Or maybe I was getting used to having pain move in and out of my bones like restless tourists.

During those weeks I learned to pray. Except for promptings by our pastor and nuns, my prayers had been mostly supplications sprinkled with childish distractions. Now, stripped of all artifices and faced with the blunt reality of invalidism, I turned to God and His Blessed Mother for the strength each day required.

I no longer offered pain halfheartedly to God through the aspiration, "All for Thee, my Jesus!" Now Monday's combined aches and confinement were offered to God through our Lady for the agony her Son endured in Gethsemani; Tuesday, for His scourging before Pilate; Wednesday, His crowning with thorns; Thursday, the journey to Calvary; Friday, the wounds caused by the nails; Saturday, His sword-pierced side; Sunday, His death. Not until later was I to understand more fully the need and the value of suffering, but at least I had become aware that I was sharing in a great and powerful mystery.

A single branch outside my window kept me posted on the progress spring was making. A bird interrupted its flight to pause there a moment. Then Easter, the symbol of hope, gave me a brief respite from hospital routine. For one precious week my casts and I were home. Because I had not learned to accept these reprieves for what they were instead of what I wished them to be, returning to the hospital was always a readjustment.

I had long dreaded to face my class's graduation from high school; yet it came and passed with only a fraction of the anticipated regret. When they visited me on their Skip Day, I had the strange feeling that all we now shared were memories and an Alma Mater. For somewhere in my months away from them, our interests had changed. Still the meeting was not without shadows, for my inability to be graduated left me with a sense of unfulfillment that has never faded.

Summer brought a new enemy — heat. 107 degrees of it. Medics panted down the halls wearing defeated looks and wilted clothing. Weary night nurses answered uncountable call lights and prayed for fortitude when patients asked for a fan and ice chips. Wringing wet from the heat of my leather-topped steel braces, I sighed with relief as a nurse mopped my forehead and fanned a breeze under my back.

As I look back over my first year at St. Joseph's (it seems a hundred years ago!) I think of the many blessings God granted me. Without the daily reception of Holy Communion, I couldn't possibly have endured the pain. And I was fortunate in spending my first year of invalidism in a hospital rather than at home. Even to this day receiving personal care is distasteful to me. But in the hospital, a mutual understanding between patient and nurse makes this personal assistance tolerable, as though each of them knows the language of suffering. The varied nursing shifts spare the chronic patient the fear of being a burden, as he may well be in a private home where a relative performs 24-hour duty. Helpful too is the absence of that dreadful I'm-not-where-I-belong feeling. One *does* belong and is accepted casually, that is as it should be. Respect for a schedule begins to grow, and life in general becomes well-regulated, if nothing else.

Through Patricia O'Brien, a Sioux City senior whose parents once lived in Marcus, I became acquainted with other girls our age. But for the most part, hospital workers, interns and nurses made up my world. There was no question of not belonging. I was accepted as one of them — a part of the strange, complicated fabric into which I was now patterned. Petite Helen Kennedy, one of the first girls Patricia O'Brien brought to see me, became a switchboard operator at St. Joseph's after graduation. Soon she was my chief ally. On her hours off she wrote my letters, combed my hair in the latest style, and supplemented the institutional fare with coke and potato chips bought for me from her meager salary. We listened to the radio, shared secrets and marveled at being grown up.

How many and how generous were these and others who transposed my confinement from one of boredom to one of interest and learning! There was Norma, a highly intellectual laboratory technician who read to me . . . Mabel, a lovely blonde nurse who spent countless hours in my room . . . Paul, the handsome orderly who loved her and told me to look after her when he went off to war . . . "Cookie," the piano-playing intern who also loved her but lost . . . my cousin Florence Delaney, who taught me much about the fine things of life and encouraged my writing dreams . . . Nancy, the Irish food buyer who sometimes slipped me a steak or a piece of cake. And ever so many more! Only in heaven will they know how much their kindness contributed to the bearableness of my life on the horizontal during those first long weeks.

Those weeks had their tender moments, reflective ones, and also a few annoying ones . . . I'll never forget some of them: The Gray Lady, who, while reading *Kitty Foyle* aloud to me, came over to the bed to show me the swear words rather than say them . . . the visitors who always had a grandfather or an aunt-in-law with rheumatoid arthritis . . . well-wishers who advised me to "mind the doctor" or "stay right in there and pitch" . . . and nurses who closed both of my nostrils just as I blew my nose . . . or spooned up the spilled soup off my chin and then shoved it into my mouth.

CHAPTER 4

BROTHERHOOD, INC.

One day there appeared at the door of my hospital room a sober-faced priest I had never seen before. "Are you Mary Ellen Kelly?" he asked.

"Yes, but — "

"Bob Kelly's sister?"

"Yes, but — "

"Good. Just heard you were a patient. Too bad. I'm Father Preisinger of Trinity College and I've brought some boys to read to you. Would you like that? If so, they can come several afternoons a week."

Tempted to reply that I would like college boys any time, I answered "yes" to all the questions and added that the boys from Trinity would indeed be welcome.

This abrupt introduction to Trinity, which my brother had attended for one year, brought into the life of this Kelly a stream of happiness which to this very day still flows. Although it is now a minor seminary conducted by the Salvatorian Fathers, Trinity still seems vividly alive to me, personified by every boy who went to school there.

The reading sessions lasted a week. They were instructive, but just getting acquainted and talking was more fun. Each boy who came to see me was different; each offered something special. With one I seriously discussed writing; another was my Mr. Fixit. Others were jovial entertainers, and several who were shy taught me how to dig down for the real person beneath the shyness.

Every week end, rain or shine, after the first days of reading, the

Trinity boys who boarded at the school appeared faithfully, with the rest of the week ably represented by many day students. They were the nuns' despair, the nurses' delight, and my salvation.

One of them, then a seminarian, even invented an electric page turner for me. The talk of the hospital, it resembled something discarded by Rube Goldberg, but it worked! After months of no reading at all, and more months of waiting for a passerby to turn my page, it was sheer heaven to read one page after another again. To this young man, now Father Edward Carpenter, I owe an enormous debt.

One June day, shortly before summer vacations, a group of Trinity boarders marched into my room. Spokesman Stefan Halaszyn, who had become one of my dearest friends, solemnly announced that I had been named an honorary member of their fraternity, *Upsilon Kappa Upsilon.* Moved by the news, I resorted to the feminine reaction of tears. Ignoring my tears as best he could, Steve presented me with a badge of membership, a spiritual bouquet, and a poem, written and exquisitely printed by his talented hands.

In the months that followed, I often wondered why God had chosen me for a role of suffering. I wondered at times what His plan could be, but never did it occur to me to question the choice itself. For some particular reason God had permitted me to become an invalid. Might it be to atone for the sins of people whose hearts felt no contrition? Might it be the means of my own salvation? Perhaps I would never be really sure. And yet of this I was positive: *mine* was not a life of punishment nor was it being wasted. For it was dedicated to the Blessed Virgin, and she takes better care of her gifts than that.

God was generous with His blessings. I knew that even during black moments (as when rules enforced by the supervisory nun upset my happy plans). Virtually everyone who entered my room contributed to my days, whether it was to fill a lonely hour or merely to wipe my nose.

Winter's end in '41 was marked with an unprecedented event. A former Trinity friend who was working in a local mortuary asked his genial bosses, Tony and Bill Perasso, if he could take me in their ambulance to see *Gone with the Wind* at a Sioux City theater.

For this momentous event Mother came from home to accompany me, not only because of the importance of the occasion (it made page one of the Marcus *News!*), but to lend assistance just in case the long film posed any personal problems. It did, too, and no effort to insure a quiet, private intermission ever precipitated a greater convergence of managerial talent. The solicitude displayed was second only to Scarlett O'Hara's concern for Scarlett.

Around this time there came into my life a wonderful trio. At least ten times they walked past my door before the smallest of the three suddenly turned on his heel and strolled in, the other two — also around 17 or 18 — following suit.

"Hi," they said in unison.

"Hi," I replied. "Won't you sit down?"

The middle-sized one took a chair, the tall one turned the wastebasket over and sat on it, and the third, the smallest, twirled a long watch chain and declared as he paced, "Me, I'm restless."

They lived close to St. Joseph's and were viewed with favor at the Nurses Home. I had seen them go by and knew of them through the medical grapevine which made them sound halfway between the Dead End Kids and a three-headed Robin Hood. In the months that followed I learned for myself what capacities for kindness were concealed beneath their roguishness.

Standing over 6 foot 3, with close-cut, jet-black curly hair, was Howard Cheever, understandably called "Highpockets." He worked at a factory since graduating from high school and, as regularly as night succeeds day, came to see me after work. No visitor in white tie and tails would have been more welcome than Cheever in his overalls and carrying his lunch pail.

Sometimes his mother sent me along homemade doughnuts or a bouquet of flowers, and every Sunday afternoon his own gift was a pound of freshly roasted peanuts, one of my many weaknesses. The nurses shared the gift with me and would have continued to approve of this ritual if it hadn't been for my lack of will power.

But every week my overindulgence resulted in a desperate summons for help from my overtaxed stomach, and every week the summons came too late.

Jerry Coates was a more complex blend. He covered up his boyish insecurities with mimicry, loud clothes and bravado. Minus this act, he was loyal, eager to be accepted, and always ready to help.

John Knapp was the thinker; he was conservative, thorough, reliable, tender. And what an explosive giggle! No day remained somber once this infectious outburst sounded in my room.

I came to love this trio. They provided fun, excitement, companionship, and that special quality I can describe only as masculinity. They helped the nurses lift me into the wheelchair, and wheeled me outdoors. Sometimes we went to their homes; other times we sat in front of the Nurses Home or went across the street for a Coke in the neighborhood's only drugstore. There were picnics, too, where I was fed, among other things, toasted marshmallows — a task that is really not worth the effort!

These three sometimes concocted devilment that gave gray hairs to the floor supervisor and made me forget my arthritis.

One New Year's eve they came breezing in with mysterious looks on their faces. This was one of the lonesomest nights of the year, so I was happy to be included in their plans.

"Pull up a chair." I said. "There's some homemade candy on the dresser."

"We've got something better, Kelly," Jerry announced mysteriously.

Tenderly he took from his pocket a small flat bottle and held it up before me. "Feast your big brown eyes on the best likker that money — cheap money, that is — can buy."

"Jerry! Put that out of sight or we'll be shot!"

"Not till you celebrate with us! Where can we get a Coke or Seven Up?"

"Only in surgery, but you be careful." I warned.

Waiting for his return was like holding a wake. He finally appeared empty-handed and breathless.

"What happened, Jerry?"

"I've been playing hide-and-go-seek with a *nun!* I don't think she knows me, though, and I'm going to keep it that way! This kid's too young to die!"

A bit of spirited beverage would have indeed added a festive note to my otherwise solitary and arid vigil, but the boy had made a gallant try and that's what counted. However, the revelers, insistent on my being witness, at least, to some kind of toast, had an idea that would cause no noise or keep them past bell time. Quietly — over my protests — they carried out their plan. The next morning, floating in my fish bowl were four very dead guppies. They had been saluted and embalmed with the "best likker money can buy."

In two years this beloved trio was war-bound and not for five years were we together again. On that unforgettable reunion Coates brought me another bottle — this time filled with an exquisite Parisienne perfume. From John Knapp — perfume from Belgium. From Highpockets (then not a convert) — a silver rosary, a mother-of-pearl-covered prayerbook, and a little shrine honoring the heavenly Queen who helped effect their safe return.

That same week the Good Shepherd Sisters invited me to a stage show for the girls at the Home. Trinity students bundled me up and helped Cheever and Knapp carry my chair over the snow banks and up the steep hill leading to the Home. It was no amateur production, but the Lawrence Welk Show, an orchestra popular in the midwest.

One of the entertainers that day was a young impersonator whose act brought down the house. After the show he told me he had received an invitation to entertain at the White House.

"I guess Lady Luck has finally got my number," the dark-eyed singer-mimic exclaimed.

His name was Dean Martin.

CHAPTER 5

THE HARD WAY

ONE fall day a priest visitor asked me a question that exploded in my smug little world like a well-aimed grenade.

"What do you know about meditation?"

"Meditation!" I said. "You must be joking. Anyway, it's only for nuns and priests, isn't it?"

That I was wrong became plainly evident. Only not until he finished speaking did I know just *how* wrong I was.

My caller explained that there are two types of prayer, vocal and mental. The first consists largely of prayers which are recited, both aloud and silently; also prayers which are read. While this type of prayer is indeed necessary and effective, one should not be content to limit communion with God solely within its confines.

For there is another method, he continued, which uses all three faculties of the mind — memory, will, and understanding. This method, called mental prayer, has two divisions — meditation and contemplation. "About the latter," the priest said smiling, "we won't worry for a while."

To prepare for meditation, he told me, one should try to establish within oneself a sense of quietude, and then ask the Holy Ghost for help in making a good meditation. One next selects a particular scene from the life of Christ — for example, His birth. Visualizing this scene with the powers of imagination brought sharply into play, one fills in the picture by employing first his senses — sounds heard, the chill of the stable, the smell of frankincense.

And then his intellect: *Why did Christ come on earth? Why did He choose to be born in poverty? Why had Mary and Joseph come to Judea? What does the Infant want of me?*

When these questions are answered slowly and with care, one begins to make a personal application. Sometimes, he added, this probing reveals a hollow-eyed skeleton of the spiritual life which indifference or self-love had sentenced to death.

However, these disclosures are not ends in themselves. They should serve only as a means to expose the weak spots, to become better aware of the grace needed to strengthen them and, by a greater realization of goodness and love, to lead eventually to a more perfect relationship with God.

Picking up his hat, the tall, thin priest gave me his blessing, quietly reminded me that meditation *was for all who love God*, and left.

For a long time I lay perfectly still, as though any sudden movement would destroy the room's blessed stillness. Into a part of me I didn't know existed, a door had been opened. Thus far, there was scarcely room to look in, so what I was to find therein was to remain a mystery for the present. But at least the room had been discovered and the door set ajar. Someday, with God's help, I resolved, it would be flooded with His light.

My determination and sincerity that day were probably pleasing to heaven's court, but I have often wondered since if amused glances were not exchanged when, later that same day, I put my plans and intentions into a nutshell and declared half aloud, "I am going to become a saint!"

By January, 1943, the hospital had been my home for more than a thousand days and nights. Now with many friends overseas, each separation from a loved one seemed a greater wrench than the one before. Within six weeks I had said good-by to my brother, to Cheever, Knapp, and Coates, to friends from Trinity, and to Mabel, who had married Paul at a California Army Base. I also said good-by to Helen Kennedy and Stefan Halaszyn, the Trinity student who had welcomed me into the school's fraternity. Although he was a soldier, bidding him and Helen good-by wasn't exactly a "service connected" heartache, for these two, who had met each other in my room, left as man and wife.

Before their wedding, the Sisters kindly let me give Helen a small bridal shower. Its gay moments lingered on long after the guests left, leaving me contented as I lay there in my room, dark except for the alternating red and blue neon flashes from the drugstore across the street.

Suddenly a peculiar sensation gave me a start. I looked down at my legs and saw a fat mouse shoot across the sheet and stop on my right knee. The screams that followed put the banshees to shame and scared every nurse within earshot.

It even scared the mouse. With startling take-off power, the small intruder ran up my arm and, in its haste to escape, became entangled in my pageboy bob. . . . The nurses told me later that there were two more screams. I wouldn't know; I went out like a light.

With so many friends away, I felt like three widows. My twentieth New Year's, No. 4 as a patient, showed no hint of being different from the previous three. Hospital routine was ingrained in me; its noises, smells, successes, failures, faults, and virtues made up my world. Visitors were people from another planet; they encouraged, helped, and taught me — even tried hard to understand. But sooner or later they had to leave, and I was alone. Tomorrow night and the next were all cut from the same pattern.

For the first time I felt as barren as the leafless tree outside my window. This sense of vegetating was frightening and loathesome. Solitude stimulated my imagination and gave rise to ideas I longed to put on paper. But no amount of wanting to could move my stiff fingers, and attempts to dictate writing of any kind were discouraging. Revealing thoughts before they were free from birthmarks was like receiving company with hair pinned up and cold cream on.

Perhaps this restlessness found its source in the general unrest which is war's gift. Each day's happiness depended on whether or not it brought letters from those dear to me. Spiritually, I felt neither progress nor recession, only the tasteless dryness of inertia. No feeling of depression was present, only a lethargic, despairing lassitude. Everyone around me seemed to be generating power. But not me. My inner engine limped along on one weak cylinder.

But our Lady, who is always looking over the shoulder of my soul, came to my rescue before any real damage was done. This time her blessing masqueraded as an operation — a disguise complete with the most realistic of props.

This three-act drama was, believe it or not, my idea. While my doctor was making his rounds one day I mustered enough courage to ask, "Isn't there *some* way you can fix my arm so that I can write again? It's been over two and a half years!"

"Write?" he echoed.

"Oh *yes*, Doctor. *I just have to!*"

Strong fingers examined my right elbow and shoulder.

"Well, Mary," the big man declared in his most orthopedic tones, "we might be able to send you on a little trip upstairs at that. We just might."

At that moment Mother's face came before me. As a hollow pain lowered itself deep into my insides I could hear her dear voice asking, "Honey, are you sure it's worth it?" Yes, I was sure.

A brisk command then set into action a drama in which I was silently to co-star. As soon, that is, as an X-ray machine had screen-tested me.

Act One concerned the removal of a thin muscle-covering (facia) from my left thigh. For ten days this was processed and refrigerated. For the first half of that time I wondered why on earth I had considered being able to write so all-fired imperative.

In Act Two the surgeon skillfully exposed my collarbone, which he quickly daubed an anemic red. Poised, knife in hand, he went into action. . . . Calcium deposits were slowly chiseled away from the clavicle and elbow joint. Manipulation then restored partial joint movement, facia was wrapped around the bending areas, the incision closed and a cast applied.

The second act ended. Wearily, the standing performers removed their costumes as the still silent co-star was wheeled back to her dressing room.

Act Three saw the agony of post-surgery. It did not require great talent, only an inexhaustive supply of perseverance. The pain was a hot, searing breath that reduced to ashes my arduously built inner haven known as "Capacity to Suffer." Cornell could keep the stage; all I wanted was aspirin.

The final act took place two weeks later in the patient's room. This scene I play to the hilt. The stitches were removed, and once again my arm felt as if it belonged to me. Now for the experiment's final step.

"How's the arm?" my doctor asked.

"Great!" I replied, hoping he would take my word for it and not go probing around.

"Fine. Tomorrow when I come in, I want you to be writing."

I looked at my hands. Every joint was rigid, wrists the same. They'd be a big help.

The search for equipment was successful except for the board for me to write on. At last one of the orderlies burst triumphantly into my room.

"Here you are, Kelly! Found this in an ash can. Will it do?"

One look at the board he held told me that the size was perfect, but what were those markings on it? A nurse answered my question: "Good grief — a OUIJA board!"

Quickly it was slipped under my arms, with books supporting it. One arm was placed on a towel, the other on a rolled copy of the *Woman's Home Companion*. Nervously, I nodded to the nurse who carefully placed a pen between my thumb and index finger. It felt cold and hard to my tender knuckles. Slowly my hand began to trace the alphabet, my grin widening with every letter. When I paused after "F" the onlookers chorused, "What's the matter, Kelly?"

"How in the heck do you make a capital G?"

The next day Mom and Dad received a lined post card bearing these lines:

IT WORKS!
IT WORKS!
IT WORKS!

My writing looked more like Sanscrit than the Palmer Method, but to my parents it was beautiful.

Gradually my technique improved. Within a few weeks I was answering all my own letters, and with each one the joy of unviolated privacy deepened. I still had to depend on others to fold the sheets and put them into envelopes, but this I didn't mind too much — except, that is, when the wrong combination was put together.

I became frightened several months later when my elbow stiffened again, losing all movement gained by surgery. But fortunately, enough shoulder action remained to allow my hand to make seven letters with one unbroken movement. It wasn't much, but with my left hand and the point of my pen I could move the paper and make seven more letters. The sharp angle of vision required to see what I was writing remained a minor problem until 1957, when our local optometrist suggested the addition of a prism in my reading and writing glasses. It works splendidly, elevating my paper and my line of vision considerably.

Visitors often look doubtful when they learn that I write at least eight hours a day. As one remarked, "But not even an *ordinary* person could keep that up!" Though I do indeed write at times until I ache, the process for the most part is not one requiring Herculean strength. I am in a comfortable position and have a handy writing stand; my wrist joints are so fused that there is no danger of twisting or even bumping them, and my pen fits between my thumb and finger so snugly that no real grip is necessary.

If the ability to write cost me ten times its present price, I still would pay it gladly. There are moments when I long desperately to release some emotion in a physical way. Sometimes my inability to do so is hard to bear; yet with a little time the emotion passes and, with it, the urgency to do something about it. But thoughts are different. They have a way of hanging around, leaving and returning, popping up when defenses to combat them are low. For that reason, I thank God each day of my life that I can write and release these thoughts on paper. I can't expend all the feelings that come — many get caught in a bottleneck; but as long as I can write a letter to ease loneliness for one I love, or an article that might help someone, or a column that conveys my thoughts, then I have at my finger tips a priceless treasure.

CHAPTER 6

IF NOT DELIVERED IN TEN DAYS

THE activity of spring contrasted with the decreased activity of my elbow joint. Still it didn't frighten me; even rigid, it covered a three-inch range. After months of no writing at all, I would have gladly settled for less.

But even writing palled as the heat and sameness of the summer wore on. What unleavened days they would have been without Mary Kennedy and Helen Kovarna. I called them by their last name and they called me Kelly. Mary, Helen Kennedy's youngest sister, came to work at the Nurses Home after graduation in 1941 and took over where Helen left off. Her sweet, quiet charm was complimented by long brown hair, deep blue eyes and thick black lashes, a wide, warming smile, and a doll-like figure.

In contrast was Helen Kovarna, Kennedy's tall, slender and willowy roommate. After we met in '42, she admitted having seen me two years earlier, but an unfounded feeling of shyness had kept her from coming into my room. Kovarna, the ever kind one, moved into my heart and stayed there. She shampooed my hair, kept my nails trimmed (a rather painful process), wrote letters, shopped for me, wrapped Christmas gifts, and did a hundred other things for me.

I can still see them — Cheever, Coates, Knapp, Kennedy, and Kovarna — sitting around my hospital bed. They made me one with them, so that I moved out of my teens without feeling cheated of all boy-girl relationships. To be sure, my association with boys was different from a girl's who was healthy, and yet, I have always felt proud (humbly so) to have been considered a friend of so many fine young men. It has meant a far deeper mutual sharing, also a much longer one; because once a girl marries she can hardly expect her husband to be ecstatic each time "an old friend" drops in.

In early spring of '43 Mary Jackman, the X-ray technician, entered my life. We have sometimes been taken for sisters, for we are about the same coloring and size, and both have Ireland in our freckled faces. I'm still not sure if our similarities or our differences brought us so close together.

Witty, mischievous, fun-loving, saucy, independent, an attractive dresser and good dancer, Jackman was real "date bait," and with the Sioux City Air Base a short distance away, she could have had a hundred B-17's named after her if she had decided to. Sometimes she and Kennedy double-dated, but whether they did or not, each gave me a sleepy-eyed account the next day.

More explosive than Kennedy, my X-ray companion sometimes grew furious at my seeming indifference to certain matters. Her freckles popped out, blue eyes lit up, and her pretty lips narrowed. Even if I was angry, I couldn't help laughing, because by this time I would have forgotten why she was angry.

One day Bill Perasso took us to a movie and told us to be sure to watch the Legion parade afterward. The White Horse Shrine Patrol had just passed when a well-meaning onlooker came toward me and, with a raucous greeting, picked up my hand. Jackman sent him on his way at once, but his gesture broke the adhesions in my middle finger. The pain was rough, but getting away from the crowd was rougher. Reaching the corner at last, we stopped to plan our next move when from behind us came a question that floated toward me on a bourbon mist: "Whash happened to the lady? Ish she sick?"

"No," Jackman snapped. "When she was a WAC, she was injured and had to stay on the battlefield for three days."

"Thash a gosh darn dirty shame, yes sir. . . ."

One day in July I asked the girls about going to Lake Okoboji for a week.

"Oh — oh!" Jackman said. "There goes my insurance payment."

"We could ask Tony and Bill to take us, rent an inexpensive cottage, and pool our expenses."

We did too, and with my nurse friend Mabel as our chaperone and six other girls eager to share our plan, everything was set. To help raise my share of the funds, I sold my electric clock.

On a torrid Saturday evening we left the hospital. Perasso's rig (a shorter and cheerier name than the hearse) bulged with groceries, a hot meal from Mother, and girls galore. From my wheelchair I could see the cornfields wave as we sped by. Singing everything from "Frankie and Johnny" to "Tantum Ergo," we reached our cottage in three hours.

In one sweeping gesture the stars and the night and the clean, fresh smell of the lake invited me into paradise. My heart soared to a dizzy height. I thought it had forgotten how to fly.

Wrapped in sudsy clouds and resting on a blue crest of glory are the days I spent at Okoboji. Their freedom, gaiety, beauty, and disregard for routine compensated for every dull and confining moment of my invalidism.

Next to staying up late, my chief delight was watching the lake in its changing moods. I likened it to a woman, sometimes a capricious dancer with ruffled hemline and cancan garters. Or she would be somber, reticent and still in her gray, clean gown. In this mood no one ever guessed that she could be vindictive, violent, or shrewish. But she could!

I loved our unorthodox routine. I even loved to get up early, although most of the time I had to watch the sunrises alone. Later on we played records and stuffed ourselves with inexpensive and easy to prepare food. We sang and reminisced and talked about the men in our lives, roasted under the sun and shivered under the moon. We voted Kennedy "Miss Okoboji of 1943," stayed up at night until we were numb, and became shoreline experts at sailboating.

To all this was added the joy of meeting a number of LaSalette Missionary Fathers and Brothers, who had a seminary and boys' camp across the ball field from our cottage. Meeting the LaSalettes changed my first vacation into something extra special. Meeting them even changed my life.

From the Superior to the working Brothers I was welcomed each day as several of the scholastics carted me from our cottage across their property and out onto the dock, where I watched the campers tumble up and down in clear blue water. The Brothers were kindness personified; and in all their joking, work, fun, and consideration was the sweet presence of humility. They had renounced the world and their identity; yet by some paradox they emerged as individual giants.

Being with the LaSalettes was like making a retreat in an amusement park. Although I never had more fun in my life, I felt at peace, secure, close to God. In a way I felt a similarity in our lives: like me, they had been chosen for a special job. They, too, were restricted to a rigid schedule, but where physical laws bound me, their vows of poverty, chastity, and obedience bound them. The real difference was: the Brothers knew *why* they were chosen, and when the call came, they had a choice. I had none.

Like the Blessed Mother, to whom their lives were consecrated and whose virtues they were striving to imitate, the LaSalettes communicated a sense of well-being, charity, and hopefulness that I received with all the fervor I possessed.

Fall greeted me with a smile. I smiled back. Why not? My favorite team had won the Series, and Dad came to the hospital to listen with me to the crucial games — a habit we started when I was in grade school. Even my routine had its face lifted, thanks to Tony and Bill Perasso who took me to a circus, to ball games (where I met Luke Sewell and Mickey Cochran), and to a concert by Sigmund Romberg, who, much to my surprise, dedicated the "Gershwin Cavalcade" to me.

We also attended the Ballet Russe, a Marian Anderson concert, "Blossom Time," and "The Student Prince." The starring prince, filled with a head cold, spent most of his time blowing his royal nose.

Bill Perasso took me to my first stage play, "The Corn Is Green," starring Ethel Barrymore. I was entranced by her brilliant portrayal of the school teacher, and watched her every move, scarcely seeing the others in the cast. I was no longer in Sioux City; I was in Wales.

While waiting afterward for the ambulance, my companions

pushed me down front to watch the scenery and props hauled away. I regretted being a witness to this, for it seemed to destroy all the illusions of the play. The mood was gone—

Then I noticed her. Kerplopping across the stage in a black dress, silver fox jacket and big, flapping galoshes, was Ethel Barrymore! Quickly I called a huddle. Did we dare try to intercept her at the lobby entrance? My friends didn't answer. They just acted.

Face to face with the great actress, I am sure I stared at her openly. With lips pursed and eyes squinting, she asked in her deep hoarse voice if I enjoyed the theater, and if I were sufficiently covered. She tucked the blanket more firmly under my shoulders. As she leaned over, the porcelain-white skin of her face and throat crowded together into a network of fine lace. Suddenly I was sorry that she was growing old.

The hospital's distaff side shared my next excitement. Tony Perasso, always thinking up something to surprise me, announced that he was bringing me a visitor later in the day.

"Swell," I replied. "Who?"

"Jimmy Stewart."

"Oh sure," I answered, "and tell him to bring along Clark Gable."

When he convinced me that the famous Hollywood actor, then stationed at the Sioux City Air Base, had really accepted Tony's invitation to visit me, I wasn't so flippant.

Tony asked me to keep the news secret for the star's sake (a mob of women had torn the buttons off his uniform and snatched his tie on his one and only appearance downtown). I told no one but my doctor and my three best friends, Kennedy, Jackman, and Kovarna.

The girls cleaned my room. Even the dresser drawers were laid with fresh papers (this step we regarded later in puzzlement). Then six hands made me as presentable as nature would allow, and Bill Perasso delivered a magnificent basket of mums brought directly from a funeral. Just the touch that was needed.

When the zero hour arrived, the excitement extended from the rear parking lot, where a jeep had just deposited Captain Stewart and Tony, through the corridors right up to my door. My doctor had been so pleased over my good fortune that he had confided my secret to someone else — a head nurse. She too repeated it only once — in the nurses' dining room. Consequently on the reception line were all the girls from laundry workers to the chief supervisors.

If the Hollywood idol was irked, he concealed it. His quiet friendliness put me at ease immediately. We listened spellbound as he talked on in his pleasant drawl. He patiently answered my questions. His most difficult role, he told us, had been playing the drunk in an hilarious scene in "Philadelphia Story," the role that won him an Oscar. "To be convincingly plastered while cold sober is no snap," he admitted, "especially when you're supposed to be funny. A hiccough can sound awfully phoney!"

"My favorite picture of yours is 'Seventh Heaven,' " I confided.

"Remember the scene where I carried Diane (Simone Simon) up that stairway to the attic? Well, it took six trips before the director was satisfied, and Diane, who always went completely limp, was heavier than a sack of potatoes!"

Some weeks later a large box arrived from California. In it were four volumes containing the complete works of Shakespeare in an 1886 edition replete with gold trim and wood cuts.

With the gift was this handwritten note:

"Dear Mary Ellen,

Hope you will like these — I don't read much, but I think this fellow is pretty good. I enjoyed our visit and wish you the very best of everything.

Sincerely,
Capt. Jimmy Stewart"

CHAPTER 7

SOMETHING NEW IS ADDED

ON NEW YEAR'S EVE, 1943, I met Father James L. McShane, an energetic and understanding Jesuit priest who was preaching the nurses' retreat. He asked me if I belonged to the Sodality of Our Lady.

"No," I quickly replied, "I'm not a Sodalist, and incidentally, that's a sore spot."

"I don't understand."

"It's simple," I answered. "When I was in high school we didn't have a Sodality, so there was no chance of becoming a member before arthritis nosed into the picture. The Nurses' Sodality isn't for me — a patient — and neither am I eligible for a college Sodality or one for young married women. So where does that leave me? On the outside looking in! Frankly, Father, not being a Sodalist has been a big disappointment. There's just no place in the Sodality for people like me."

The young priest regarded me shrewdly as his Irish face crinkled into a smile. "Why don't you start one yourself?"

Later that night when I was alone in my room with the tree lights diffusing Yuletide glow, I felt strangely excited. A plain-spoken stranger had plunked a challenge into my lap. To ignore it would be cowardly; to accept it would be laying myself wide open for worry, work, and disappointments. I looked across the room to a picture of the Madonna and asked, "What would you do if you were in my place, Mary?"

By the time 1944 had officially arrived, my decision was made. I would try to establish a Sodality just for invalids.

If I had known that sixteen months would pass before the National Sodality Headquarters would send final approval, my patience might not have stood the strain. I doubt too that I would have made that initial move if I had known that six months later I would be leaving the hospital. But I didn't know this then; or that research was being done at Sodality headquarters on my proposed organization. Father Daniel A. Lord, S.J., noted author, speaker, and national Sodality director, had kept me waiting until he was sure my enthusiasm was not a passing thing. Ideas, I learned later, were submitted to him by the dozens, but their originators' interest seldom outlasted the unwinding of necessary red tape.

An article about me in the April issue of *The Queen's Work*, the official Sodality magazine, resulted in a large number of letters including those from four other invalids. Three of these were rheumatoid arthritics like myself: Mary Veronica Kelley, Winner, S. Dak.; Madonna Fox, Woonsocket, R. I.; and Dixie MacMaster, Montreal, Canada. The other girl, Betty O'Brien, Newark, N. J., was a victim of cerebral palsy. Each of these girls' letters revealed qualities that made me both eager to answer their letters and seek their friendship.

When I told them later of my plan, their interest so encouraged me that I invited these new friends to share in the Sodality's formation. Together we defined the purpose of our embryo apostolate:

> "To unite the sick, aged, and disabled in prayer and suffering for the honor and glory of God and the sanctification of their own souls.
>
> "To foster in our members an ardent devotion to the Blessed Mother and to attain through the help of her Sodality a more intimate union with Christ Crucified.
>
> "To show our members the value, need, and power of illness and deformity; to bring the sick encouragement and comfort, and to acquaint the afflicted with each other."

These aims were to be promoted through a bimonthly periodical which I suggested we call *Seconds Sanctified*. My job would be to edit and publish this paper, with articles solicited from the members. Ready to assume the role of spiritual adviser was Rev. T. J. Schulte, S.J., of Denver's Regis College. This jovial priest, to whom

Father McShane was deeply devoted, had been forcibly retired by the amputation of both legs. He ably qualified for this office as he knew the problems and distress of confinement to a wheel chair.

We then defined the requirements and drew up the "Seven Promises" which soon received ecclesiastical approval. These each new member would be asked to make. They were as follows:

1. To be resigned to God's will in sickness and in health.
2. To consecrate one's sufferings and disappointments daily to our Lady in union with, in reparation for, and in loving honor of, the Passion and Death of her Son.
3. To set aside one day each month in special honor of Our Lady of Fatima, our patroness.
4. To spend fifteen minutes a day in mental prayer, and as much time or more in spiritual reading; to say a Hail Mary for *The Queen's Work* staff.
5. To say a rosary each week for peace and for the conversion of Russia.
6. To dedicate the four Sundays of the month as follows:
   SICK SUNDAY: for the sick and dying, especially for sick Sodalists.
   MISSION SUNDAY: for those laboring in mission fields and for all priests everywhere, especially those who remember us in their daily Mass, that they may garner a great host of souls for Christ.
   HOLY FATHER SUNDAY: for the personal and general intentions of Pope Pius XII, our fellow Sodalist.
   ALL SOULS' SUNDAY: for the souls in Purgatory, prisoners, the oppressed, weak converts, and fallen-away Catholics.
7. To recite daily St. Francis of Assisi's prayer for peace.

At long last, word came from Father McShane that the National Sodality Headquarters had given the green light! One final step was to be taken. With my heart racing I wrote the Most Reverend Edmund Heelan, Bishop of Sioux City, to ask his permission to establish this apostolate in his diocese. On April 13, 1945, his approval was given and the League of Shut-In Sodalists pushed up its sleeves and started to work.

To my deep regret, Bishop Heelan lived to see only three years of the League's development. From its humble beginning, when a neighboring Swedish Lutheran minister mimeographed thirty-five copies of *Seconds Sanctified*, it has expanded far beyond my original dream. Today three thousand copies roll off the press at each printing. Its message is read in fifty states and thirty-six countries: Arabia, Argentina, Australia, Canada, England, Ireland, Scotland, Germany (even the Russian zone), Malta, Italy, France, Holland, Portugal, Spain, India, Japan, the Philippines, China, Paraguay, Panama, Puerto Rico, Nyasaland, Lebanon, Liberia, Burma, Madagascar, Brazil, Mexico, Pakistan, Peru, New Zealand, B.W.I., Tanganyika, and Kenya.

Enrolled in Our League are twenty-five hundred sick and disabled men, women, and children whom I have come to love, respect, and worry about as if they were my own family. Their illnesses include tuberculosis, cancer, multiple sclerosis, muscular dystrophy, heart and respiratory ailments, dermatitis, leukemia, diabetes, elephantiasis, glaucoma, and Bright's, Parkinson's and Hansen's diseases. Also enrolled are people suffering handicaps that result from congenital deformities, injuries, accidents, and nervous disorders. Whether five or ninety-five, immobile or palsied, white or black, Catholic or Protestant, a person is welcome to become a member, providing he is willing to adhere to the rules as best he can. After all, we are all in the same boat.

Correspondence is urged among the members, who are introduced through *Seconds Sanctified;* and available without cost to the members are books from the League's library in my home. Maintaining the membership and subscription lists, stencils, index cards, postal permits, library, a bimonthly letter and our paper has become my life.

Sharing in the lives of these invalids brings strange and awesome results. I sympathize with them in their trials, and rejoice in their triumphs. By pooling our suffering, our sacrifices merge into one vast sea which is poured daily by our Lady into a great golden chalice and lifted in love and reparation to almighty God. By the same token, the weight of our individual crosses is lightened, for they are measured on a supernatural scale which regulates the burden to the grace each one is given to carry.

Problems? Almost constantly. In its years of existence (the richest years of my life), the League of Shut-Ins has transformed the Kelly household into a pressroom, book shop, and business office. Whenever I am complimented for this work for the sick, I think of Mother. My activities have invaded her privacy, upset her schedule, cluttered her house, frayed her nerves, and robbed her of rest. In crucial moments, when the paid help fails to show up, she does their work. Without her, the League would have died in infancy.

Finances are always a problem, since the enrollment itself is free. To make *Seconds Sanctified* available to the poorest of shut-ins, its annual subscription was only fifty cents until 1955, when we had to double that fee or sing a swan song. The increase has helped some, but our members in county and state institutions cannot afford even that amount, and our overseas subscribers can rarely send an offering, because of foreign exchange. I refuse to drop any delinquent invalid subscriber from our list, so there is always a deficit. Until we recently stapled our publication, more than 20,000 envelopes were used in one year. This is only *one* item.

Though never in the clear for more than a day at a time, our new world-wide apostolate consigns its worries and errors to the care of its patroness, Our Lady of Fatima, and confidently continues its work. After all, at its very conception I told Mary that the finances were to be her department. I have never had any knack for arithmetic.

Often the work weighs heavily on me; often my arm and hand ache from writing. But I have never regretted the decision made that New Year's Eve in 1943. My efforts have been well compensated. Imagine the rewarding joy I found in the following words from a letter written December 8, 1953, by a member who was shut in not only by tuberculosis, but also by prison walls:

"You remember a year ago, Mary Ellen, when everyone thought I was going to die and I thought so too! I weighed 87 pounds then. Yesterday I was over to the hospital and weighed 170! Isn't that something? If anyone had told me I would ever get this fat, I'd thought they were nuts. I began to gain right after I got all those Christmas cards and letters last year from your shut-ins. They said they all offered prayers for me and their prayers sure helped. A job is waiting for me, and soon I hope to be turned loose. No matter what comes, I'll always be grateful."

I try to inspire the afflicted, and yet more frequently I am the one who is inspired. Here is a letter from a young man in southern Europe who suffers from the fearsome pain and disfigurement of Hansen's disease:

"I wish to tell you that I have again been bedridden with acute pain of the bones and nerves through all my body. Thanks to God, I am fairly well now.

"One word more to express the heavenly bliss which I feel every time *Seconds Sanctified* reaches me. It is my true friend who sincerely speaks to me with affectionate words, and I count that his words are a treasure of gold. A shut-in who wants to excavate gold from this mine, needs only to dig into the literature of this journal, for gold is surely found there in the suffering of the shut-ins.

"It is a great pleasure for me to look at the photographs of other disabled; their fine and laughing faces make this patient accept his cross more willingly and, from his bed of sorrows, cry on the tip of his voice, the words FIAT VOLUNTAS TUA!"

PART 2

CHAPTER 8

THE PRODIGAL RETURNS

IN JULY, 1944, just when my project for invalids was beginning to show promise, I was dismissed from the hospital. For the first few days at home I basked in the novelty of low ceilings, gay wallpaper, and home cooking; it was wonderful after five years of institutional life. And then came the adjustments.

After a few days the peaceful quiet became appalling silence. Like ghostly visions from a dimly remembered Halloween were the scenes that surrounded me. With them my life was no longer compatible — arthritis had seen to that — for these were scenes representing unimpaired muscle and limb. This was a community whose homes were managed by women who worked hard, whose schools were attended by rosy-cheeked youngsters. Stores were operated by men who put in ten hours a day, six days a week. Broad cornfields were planted, cultivated, and watched over by wind-reddened farmers with strong, thick fingers. Once, like them, I too had belonged. Now I felt as out of place as a pot roast at a fish fry.

Although certain aspects of hospital life were unpleasant, I found myself missing its busy routine, its medical jargon, and the many lives that touched mine day after day. Jackman, Kennedy, and Kovarna came to see me as often as they could. Much as I loved their visits, they seemed a poor substitute for the blow-by-blow account of their lives which I had received for so long.

I couldn't blame loneliness on unfriendly treatment; I couldn't tell myself that everyone had changed. No, no one was different but me; in fact, as far as adult friends and the town itself were concerned, five years had been as the wink of an eye. But not with me. In that span of time I had changed emotionally, mentally, and spiritually.

While classmates were having their first dates, I was having my first operation. When girl friends were switching from saddle shoes to high heels, the doctors were switching me from casts to braces. And while school chums were signing marriage licenses, I was learning how to write again. Because these Marcus friends had shared none of these changes with me, I felt set apart from them and their interests. One might think that I was eager to alter this situation, but the truth is that I was afraid to. Those familiar faces and scenes were too closely linked with my pre-hospital activities which illness had so thoroughly scuttled. In short, they represented the past, and I had no desire to look in that direction.

And then history seemed to repeat itself. Again when I was feeling stranded and alone, three fun-loving, lovable characters came into my life. Bounded is a more accurate term, for Roger Rae, Leon Wallin, and Jimmy Meuhl — old Marcus highschoolers — had energy to throw away, and this returned patient was ready and willing to don a catcher's mitt. Though five years younger, they were completely indifferent to my seniority and treated me in a manner that was partly fraternal, partly protective, and wholly wonderful.

Like Cheever, Knapp, and Coates, this tireless trio carted me to ball games, dances, and movies, took me on picnics and pushed me to parties.

One evening Roger, Leon, and Jimmy took me to a friend's New Year's Eve party on the other side of town. There was the difficulty of pushing my cot through the snow drifts, but with a gesture indicating their deftness at handling just such problems, they helped Mom lift me onto the cot and soon we were on our way.

"You should rest," I warned the puffing threesome at two-block intervals.

"Relax, girl," Roger answered. "You were never in better hands."

"That may be," I replied, "but if you collapse from overexertion, don't expect me to pick you up!"

We made it at last, and the party was worth the struggle. But when the stroke of 1 A.M. reminded us of the return journey, we exchanged doubtful looks.

"I've got it!" cried Leon. "The toboggan!" Turning to our hostess he asked, "You still have it, don't you?"

"Yes, but it hasn't been waxed in years."

"Trifles, mere trifles. C'mon men, lend your muscles!"

In no time the grinning boys were back, carrying the toboggan into the basement recreation room. Carefully they lifted my cot on the elongated sled. Abruptly, their smiles disappeared. The wheels of my cot extended out beyond the sled.

"Nuts!" my escorts chorused. Roger gave Leon and Jim a reproving look. "Wait!"

He darted into the laundry room and returned a moment later with two pails which he placed on the toboggan. It wasn't hard for me to guess what he had in mind.

"Are you game?" he asked me.

"It beats walking."

While Jimmy and Leon lifted me, Roger set the overturned pails on the toboggan; then my cot was placed on the pails. The plan looked promising. Now to try it on the snow packed road. It did not strike me as an ideal mode of travel, but at least there was only a little way to fall.

We reached the road, and the boys put me down and prepared for the take-off. With Jimmy at the rear, Leon lending side protection and Roger at the helm, everything was ready. In an attempt to accent the northwoodsy scene, Roger delved into his dim recollection of Yukon tales and bellowed what he thought was a mighty command to the Huskies: "Chow! Chow!"

When the boys acted on Roger's signal for a flying start, the long unused toboggan refused to budge. The moment a little extra pull was applied, it took off with a jerk and down I went. When I had been put back onto my cot, we trekked for home somewhat less exuberantly, as the town slept.

Among others who helped me build my third world was a gentle mannered man named Ed Delaney, who owned and operated the town's only theater, the *Lyric*. Ever since the days of Our Gang comedies and Saturday night serials, I had been one of Ed's best customers. Some movies I even saw twice, thanks to his wife Kathryn, who let me in free on the second evening.

At times when I was home for a brief stay, Ed had removed some of the seats to make room for my wheelchair. No one in Marcus had a better seat at the Lyric. Now that I was again a permanent resident, he presented me with a lifetime pass which often prompted my faithful escorts to remark that taking me out had its advantages: the expense never exceeded their means.

When the Lyric burned to the ground nine years later, I cried, and my tears were partly selfish ones. My sympathy for Ed and his grand family was sincere, but my heart also felt a personal loss, as if a very happy part of my childhood had been reduced to ashes.

A number of people helped me to adjust to my new life, and of them no one more than my parents. After Mom finished with my personal care each morning, Dad helped her lift me up on the backrest and then took over. First he carried his "tool chest" (my cosmetics box) to the right side of my bed, set it on a table and solemnly raised the lid. With feigned concentration he selected powder, puff, lipstick, and a Kleenex tissue. Then brandishing the puff with a flourish, he "put on my face," as he came to call this daily procedure.

"There now!" Dad would conclude. "No one will ever recognize you!"

"Would you get the comb, Mike?" I sometimes ventured cautiously.

"Oh, no, you don't!" he would laugh. "Call your mother. That's her department!"

It was also his job at night to cover me with a blanket. With mock concern he made peaks over my feet in order to protect my toes from the weight of the blanket. He would kiss me soundly, then declare on his way to the stairs, "Good night, kid. If you need anything, don't call."

Holding the mail for me to read was another task that fell to my father's patient hands. An extremely calm man, he seldom protested against long letters or tried to hurry me.

But one day he held a letter from a woman who had read of my "condition" and wished to exchange notes on our respective creaking joints. At great length she described her symptoms and then extolled the virtues of a homemade remedy which was a "sure cure" for virtually everything from arthritis to loose dentures. After two long pages of this she concluded with a recipe for making the brew.

"Isn't this book ever coming to an end?" asked Dad.

"I've just reached it, Mike — oops — there's a P.S. on the back."

Dad turned the page with a sigh and I read aloud these final words:

"P.S. This is also good for piles."

To say that my parents had adjustments to make, too, to my being part of the Kelly ménage is a tremendous understatement. They consented to my selling Christmas cards, as I had done in the hospital, and the result was the busiest Yuletide season they had ever known.

When told of my intention to write a column for the Marcus News, they shrugged dubiously and said, "Go to it." But when young and enterprising Bernard Chicoine offered me a sizable discount on paint and wallpaper, I decided to try selling those products.

"But, Mary Ellen," Mother argued in defense. "You don't even know *how* to measure a room for paper!"

"Sure I do! Just take the length times the height and divide by thirty. That gives you the number of single rolls required." I hoped my tone sounded convincing and that Mother wouldn't ask me how to measure a room with a sloped ceiling.

Later, it was the same Bernie who wrangled Mom's permission to paint our house — a large frame structure with three stories. As I could now buy paint wholesale, it was too good an opportunity to pass by, he pointed out; besides, he claimed it was one way he could get in on Mom's cooking.

He started the job one hot Saturday afternoon with four ex-Trinity helpers. After one hour of scraping paint (a 20-year-old coat), the whole crew disappeared and didn't show up again for three days. Since it was a gratis job, we could hardly complain.

If you saw our house today, you would want to compliment Bernie and the other boys who aided him. In fact, you probably wouldn't even notice that the second story is still waiting for the second coat.

Next, a kitten named Casey entered our lives. Golden red, soft, furry, and wholly unpredictable, he captured my heart the moment the boys who found him dropped him into my lap. To his presence, Dad maintained a strictly noncommittal attitude. Robert liked him at a distance — say fifty miles — and Mother — well — that depended on Casey's behavior. The day he foundered himself on the roast beef that was to be our Sunday dinner, his rating was low. But when he curled up beside her in the rocking chair, his rating went up.

When Casey was younger, he demonstrated his agility by leaping onto my bed, a practice Mother had always discouraged, because I couldn't put him off. But one evening while reading I decided to enjoy his furry warmth against my ankle. I did too, until his curiosity led him to my adjustable book stand.

My stand flattened like a pancake the second his haunches chose it for a resting place. I yelled as the cold hard metal pressed down on my hands underneath. With the combined weight of the book, stand, and Casey on them, I'd soon have sorry-looking knuckles to explain to my mother. But as he blinked up at me sleepily, I suddenly discounted the consequences. It was nice holding something in my arms, even a cat.

And so did my life as a home patient take shape. It would be impossible to name everyone who contributed to the rebuilding, and yet the boys of the Trinity College deserve a special mention. I feared that my not being in Sioux City would mean fewer visits from them, but such wasn't the case. Sometimes they came in pairs, sometimes by the carload. Sometimes they stayed only an hour; at other times my parents thought they would never leave.

"This kindness can't keep up, honey," Dad often prophesied, "because people just aren't made that way. It's better to realize it and be prepared than to be hurt and surprised when the time comes."

As my father advised, I prepared myself. But as yet the time hasn't come. Instead, the months that followed brought even more friendships. They can't all be listed, but I am grateful to each one who imparted to my life some measure of excitement, fun, wisdom, companionship, encouragement, and inspiration.

CHAPTER 9

IN WALKED ADVENTURE

"Do you like to travel?" Father McShane asked me one day.

"I haven't had enough experience to find out," I answered. "I'm sure I would, though. Why?"

"How would you like a trip to Canada to Ste. Anne de Beaupre's Shrine?"

"Oh, by all means," I retorted. "Make it two trips — they're small."

Even though Father McShane finally convinced me that he was serious, I felt a queer and exciting sense of unreality. Later that spring night when everything was still, I pictured the adventure which, according to our Jesuit friend, was mine for the taking.

The trip was to be a spiritual pilgrimage under the direction of a Chicago travel group named the Confraternity of Pilgrims. Headed by Patrick W. O'Grady, a Notre Dame graduate of 1903, it was initiating in July an event unprecedented in the annals of commercial travel: a pilgrimage of invalids. Nurses would be in attendance, special Pullman cars chartered, Canada's three major shrines on the itinerary, and as the spiritual director there would be His Excellency, Francis J. Beckman, Archbishop of Dubuque.

All this was being offered me, Father McShane explained, because an unnamed benefactor wished to do this for an invalid in thanksgiving for a favor received. I was to get in touch with a designated party if the idea appealed to me.

Appealed to me! For days it was all I could think about until an even more incredible thing happened. William T. White, publisher of the Chicago *Herald American*, learned from his secretary, whose sister was teaching in Marcus, that I intended to make the journey alone, with only the care of the attending nurses. Immediately he instructed his secretary to send me a check that would not only cover my expenses but also my mother's. When the news reached us, Mother collapsed into the nearest chair while Dad scratched his bald head and muttered, "Well, I never!" I accepted Mr. White's offer because it enabled Mother to accompany me. But to that first anonymous would-be donor, I shall ever be grateful.

Our household routine was blown to bits. My wardrobe of sheets and blouses was carefully scrutinized and hurriedly enlarged. Robert sent me some costume jewelry from Milwaukee, and a friend gave a home permanent. The big problem was the ambulance cot. For a short visit the wheelchair provided me with sufficient rest and comfort, but after twenty-four hours of complete recline, the pillows on the spring-less woven frame soon developed rocks — or so it seemed. But once again those darlings, the Perasso brothers of Sioux City, lent me a cot which my dad polished within an inch of its life. Then our local undertaker gave me the use of his foam rubber mattress. Regardless of what lay ahead, I was assured of being well-cushioned.

Because the subject was one that made us choke up, my family and I seldom discussed the possibility of my being cured at Ste. Anne's Shrine — perhaps it was too close to our hearts to put into words. At night I wondered in the enfolding darkness about the questions for which daylight held no answer: *If I would be cured, what kind of job could I get? How would I look in a dress? Would my legs be deformed? Would the scars show on my shoulder, elbow, and leg? How could I leave the folks after all they had done for me? Would arthritis ever return, crippling me a second time? What would happen to the League of Shut-Ins? Would I be a stranger to the friends who had known me only as an invalid?*

Mother and I had crossed into Illinois before my insides settled down. With us was an added reason for my happiness — Mary Veronica Kelley, the South Dakota arthritic and charter member of the League. This was her first long trip since she had changed to a wheel chair ten years earlier, and her excitement and anticipation equaled mine. Now while she expended some of her stored-up energy in a bridge game with her companions, I watched the raindrops cling to the train window until their tails got caught in the downward current

Thanks to Mr. O'Grady, who had thought of every detail, we were met at the Chicago station by Firemen O'Connor and Cahill and transported in a spanking new fire-department ambulance to a hotel, where my brother and pilgrimage officials joined us. When the latter left at midnight, I had an idea. "Robert, how about giving me a look at Michigan Boulevard?"

"You mean push you?"

"How else?"

He grinned at Mother. "And will you take my other arm, Mrs. Kelly?"

Chicago was wearing its moon low that night, almost like a corsage. I stared at the traffic zooming by on Michigan Boulevard (the first time I had seen more than a two lane highway) and at the buildings silhouetted against the sky. From Lake Michigan came a cool breeze, and from my brother's eyes the warm reassurance of his love.

It had been a long time since the three of us had strolled along a street together; indeed a world war had taken place in the interim. I thought of that other street back in Marcus. How different it was from this mighty highway stretching out before us! Watching my brother made me wonder what our relationship would be like if I were to return on my own feet, no longer a cripple. The thought tantalized me. I imagined my brother and me dancing again, going out, discussing clothes, meeting his bachelor friends. . . .

"Are you about ready, young lady, to call it a day?" Robert asked, interrupting my thoughts.

"No, I'm not, but I'll go along quietly."

Our train was to leave the Dearborn station at 7 P.M. the next evening. Newsmen from all the Chicago papers, Associated Press, Acme News, and Time were there to photograph and cover this first national pilgrimage. As police stood duty among the crowd of onlookers, Confraternity officials assisted the wheel-chair travelers aboard the train. My cot and I were left to the last. A dozen or more men converged about me, their unsmiling faces suggesting that all was not well.

"Her cot's too wide!" one man shouted. "It will never pass *through* that window!"

"Then remove the window!" snapped another.

"Ya can't!" cried a third.

With a smile that failed to reassure me, one of the officials explained that I would have to be taken off my stretcher and passed through the drawing room window, as my unbending bones prevented entrance through the door. Without waiting for a reply, six stalwart gentlemen gently lifted me off my cot. . . . I took one look at the yawning mouth of the window above me and closed my eyes tight. There isn't a chance in the world of falling! I told myself sternly. But for some reason my pounding heart failed to get the message.

Coming out of the window in Montreal was not quite so terrifying, perhaps because the arms of six handsome French firemen maneuvered it. A waiting ambulance soon sped us through the city's bumpy brick streets and up the steep hill leading to the massive Oratory of St. Joseph, elegantly crowning the top of Mount Royal.

The ceremonies were held in the crypt chapel that houses the vault-like tomb of Canada's beloved Brother Andre. Before the huge altar, the invalids and their companions offered silent prayers of praise and thanksgiving. Later, following a sermon by Archbishop Beckman and Benediction of the Blessed Sacrament, a priest carrying the Monstrance came down through the aisles where the cots and wheel chairs were assembled. Solemnly he blessed the sick one by one while another priest called out the supplications we repeated:

"Lord, that I may walk! . . . Lord, that I may see! . . .
Lord, that I may hear! . . . Lord, heal me!"

Pride gave way to tears as heads bowed in unashamed surrender to the emotion which overcame us.

At Cap-de-la-Madeleine we came upon a different kind of splendor in the relatively small shrine of Our Lady of the Rosary. Serenity and peace hovered like a low-hanging cloud from the centuries-old church through the shaded grounds, across the Rosary Bridge right down to the river bank. Only the St. Lawrence, a broad, silvery ribbon under the sun, seemed restless.

Inside the chapel dwelt the most enveloping peace. Beauty, too, was present in the carved wooden altar, shining like polished gold and banked with tall spikes of pink, white, and blue delphiniums.

This tribute to Our Lady of the Rosary was built in 1659 on a little cape that juts out into the St. Lawrence east of the town of Three Rivers. The first church was founded by those heroic Jesuits — Marquette, Brebeuf, Daniel, and Lallement — and later placed in the care of the diocesan clergy. Unfortunately, a period of 100 years passed before the parish had another pastor. When the spirit of faith was again revived, the need for a larger church became imperative.

For two years the men of the parish cut stone on the opposite side of the St. Lawrence, planning to haul it across when the river was frozen. But the weather remained so mild that not once did ice form on the swift current. On March 15, after almost all hope was gone, a wind came up that churned the freezing waters into great ice floes. A few hours later the wind drove these cakes from along the shores to the center of the river where a bridge was formed. By now the entire parish had gathered and, while women prayed, the men quickly reinforced the bridge of ice until it was strong enough to haul the stone over it. The moment the last sled had crossed safely, the bridge of ice collapsed.

In thanksgiving, the pastor kept the old chapel intact, renovated it, moved an exquisite statue of Mary to a niche above the main altar, and rededicated it to Our Lady of the Rosary. On the evening of the ceremonies the pastor, a visiting priest, and a sick man saw the statue open its downcast eyes.

When I looked up at this same statue for the first time I gasped. On Mary's shoulders rested a blue mantle, on her head a crown of fabulous jewels. Her arms were outstretched in a gesture that encompassed each of us in a maternal embrace. Entwined about the four golden pillars of the niche was a huge rosary and beneath the Virgin's feet, the head of the serpent. Never before had it been so easy for me to lay the innermost longings of my soul at Mary's feet. For I knew that no one else would intercede for me with more fervor; no one else was as eager to teach me the full meaning of my cross; no one else was more willing to help me carry it.

The Basilica of Ste. Anne de Beaupre appeared before us through the train window as though it had sprung from the ground. Mary Veronica and I were lifted quickly from our compartment, placed in our respective wheel chair and cot, and wheeled up the winding ramp leading into the shrine. A moment later we were swallowed up in the largest church I had ever seen. Down and down into its interior my cot was pushed until I was brought to a stop before the statue of the saint I had come to venerate. There, waiting to greet me with arms outstretched was Ste. Anne, our Lord's own grandmother.

Behind the statue countless crutches, canes, and braces told of cures which had been granted. I glanced about in awe, then knew momentary panic when an unexpected thought asked: *Why should I be cured? I am only one of many who have made this long journey in the hope of being restored to health, so why should my petition be given preference? Since when did I deserve such consideration or have any right to expect it?* Not sure of the answer, I quickly recalled a prayer that asks for the desire to do God's will, and left the matter to be settled at another time.

My dreams of being well once more were such beautiful dreams that I was afraid of the disappointment that might come if I had to return home on my cot. I was afraid too of the years to come, of pain, more surgery, of endless dependence. I thought of Dad's sadness when he would see that I was still crippled. But this much I determined: whatever disappointment would come, I would not let it make me bitter. Besides, the day was not yet over nor had the time for miracles passed. Anything could happen.

The feast day ended with the candlelight procession which began at dark as thousands assembled on the hill opposite the Basilica. We invalids watched the scene unfold from the infirmary adjoining the shrine.

They came, those devotees of Ste. Anne, walking four abreast, carrying lighted candles and singing her praises as the line marched up the hill. By the time the leaders of the procession were again back to the foot of the hill, a huge S was formed on the terraced slope, a constantly moving S, ablaze with thousands of flickering candles. Slowly the procession passed our window on its way into the Basilica. I joined it there just as the canopied statue of the saint was carried in on the shoulders of an honor guard and preceded by an escort of *Les Zouaves,* alert and reverent, in uniforms of red and gray.

When the people had filed into the pews, the beating of the drums stopped and the lights were turned off, leaving only the lighted candles which were lifted in praise with each chorus of the Magnificat in a salute to God, the Source of all Light.

Suddenly a great weakness came over me, a kind of supreme exhaustion that left me limp. And with it the disappointment and heartache I had expected. But I knew without any doubt that both it and the weariness would fade in time. It was clear to me now that God wanted me to remain an invalid. I repeated these words, and when I found that they held no bitterness, the fears of the future dissolved there at the feet of the great saint.

CHAPTER 10

BRIGHTEN THE CORNER

IRRITATIONS are disguised opportunities for meriting grace. I am aware of this and try, as my mother always urges, to "offer them up for the Poor Souls." But since certain annoyances try my patience to the breaking point, I am going to keep them to myself no longer, but respectfully submit them to the good Lord, without whose help they would have driven me completely looney.

From visitors who pinch my tender toes and blandly ask, "Can you feel this?" *O Lord, deliver me!*

From hair combers who forget that I have ears, *O Lord, deliver me!*

From guests who keep asking if I am tired when I can scarcely answer for yawning, *O Lord, deliver me!*

From lumpy mattresses, wrinkled sheets, and toast crumbs, *O Lord, deliver me!*

From feeders who hold each spoonful of food above my mouth in the manner of coaxing a puppy to sit up and beg, *O Lord, deliver me!*

From feeders who stir my potatoes and gravy into a pasty mound, blow on my soup, set crackers in the pickle juice, and remove the water glass from my lips after each swallow, *O Lord, deliver me!*

From strangers who insist that my condition was caused by a faulty diet, damp climate, a lack of alfalfa, dry climate, an excess of bone marrow, or an arthritic grandfather, *O Lord, deliver me!*

From optimists who swear I'll be cured if I carry a potato in my pocket, wear a copper wire around my wrist, follow a weird diet of herbs and tea, give up salt, drink bitter vegetable juices, rub lubricating oil on my joints, take vitamin-packed mud baths, or try a remedy that brought relief to a relative — usually a deceased one — *O Lord, deliver me!*

Against the nosey who ask if I have bed sores, and the doubtful who find my negative answer difficult to believe, *O Lord, deliver me!*

Against the unthinking who interrupt my immobile discomfort just long enough to deplore the heat, recount a restless night of tossing and turning, and then hurry off to keep a swimming date, *O Lord, help me to hold my tongue in cheek!*

Against advocators of the Keep Your Chin Up, Keep Smiling, and Keep A Stiff Upper Lip philosophy, *O Lord, protect me!*

Against the overly sympathetic who pat my head and tch-tch-tch sadly, "You poor little thing!" *O Lord, protect me!*

Against the patronizing who dismiss my work with the smug remark, "It's so nice that you have something to help you pass the time away," *O Lord, deliver me!*

Against nurses who breeze into the room, ask cheerily, "Are we ready for our shot?" lay bare an unsuspecting area, thrust a long dull needle into a muscle and then cluck, "There we are!" *O Lord, protect me!*

Against the unimaginative and naïve who ask, "Don't you ever get tired of lying there?" . . . "How do you stand it — year after year?" . . . "Don't you ever lose patience?" . . . "Isn't the hair all worn off the back of your head?" . . . "How in the world do you manage to keep from being — that is — I suppose you have to eat a lot of prunes?" *O Lord, protect me!*

If my litany has given you the idea that I think all handicapped persons are without faults, it wasn't intentional. I am personal proof that they are not. Besides, those who care for invalids could probably write a litany of their own. I receive some 2000 letters a year from men, women, and children who have nearly every known illness and disability. Most of the letters are inspiring; those that are not provide the reason for a League of Shut-Ins.

From my own struggles and from my work with other invalids, I see people like us divided into different categories — some favorable, some not — just like the hale and hardy. With the usual exceptions, the majority fall into eight groups:

1. The "So-I-Had-A-Tough-Break — So-What? — So-Have-A-Lot-Of-People" type.

2. The "I've-Been-Anointed-Eleven-Times-And-I-Still-May-Go-At-Any-Moment" type.
3. The "Must-You-Do-Everything-Wrong?" type.
4. The "Don't-Open-The-Blinds — The-Sun-Might-Come-In" type.
5. The "What-Did-I-Do-To-Deserve-This?" type.
6. The "Don't-Call-Me-An-Invalid! — I'm-Merely-Handicapped!" type.
7. The "Everybody-Hates-Me-Nobody-Loves-Me" type.
8. The "With-God's-Help-I-Can-Make-This-A-Good-Life" type.

Number 4 provokes me most because there is no reason to shut out the sun and all else that is bright, happy, and normal. The room as well as the occupant becomes sour and stale, and visitors are soon repelled. And when anyone starts being left alone day in and day out, his interests become dwarfed, while perplexities and problems become exaggerated. Poor Number 3, the eternal complainer, can't even please himself.

Number 6 is asking for trouble, because he is stressing what he is being called rather than what he is. Keeping one's pride is an admirable quality, but it should take second place to humility.

But of these eight groups I feel sorriest for numbers 5 and 7, because they are both fooling and cheating themselves.

Whatever the category, I believe that with a little honest effort, we disabled could improve ourselves. Improvement must start from the inside, but presupposing for the moment that this has been accomplished, I would like to state ten tried and true "don'ts" guaranteed to help invalids (and the merely handicapped) achieve that improvement:

1. Don't allow your pain or restrictions to excuse you from observing the social graces — especially consideration, courtesy, and appreciation.
2. Don't think you are the only person in the world with an aching heart. The patient in the next bed or next block might make your troubles seem like childish imaginings.
3. Don't nag, gripe, whine, cry, pester, belittle, berate, or intimidate.

4. Don't take unfair advantage of your condition, especially by arousing sympathy.
5. Don't let the seeming indifference of the healthy make you bitter. They have their crosses too.
6. Don't forget that you have a place in the scheme of things, but remember to keep that place and not overstep.
7. Don't become lax about your appearance. Put your best foot forward — even if you aren't going to step on it.
8. Don't underestimate the value of co-operation with nurses and doctors. A little effort put forth is appreciated and capable of transforming a cold, professional attitude into one of friendly interest.
9. Don't get so set in your routine that the unexpected throws you into a "tizzy." Be more elastic toward change and you'll stretch your years into a longer, happier life.
10. Don't delude yourself into thinking that God has abandoned you or that your illness is necessarily a punishment. He permits these things to happen for a good reason, which in His own time will be revealed.

Asked one day why I bothered to use make-up, I answered not too politely, "Just because I'm no longer in the running doesn't mean I have to look like a slouch on the sidelines." A beloved nun who taught me in high school once almost prophetically advised me: "There may be days ahead when you'll forget your 'Morning Offering,' but make sure you don't forget your lipstick!"

Why do I bother? Because it makes me look better. It eliminates the pallor associated with sickness and helps friends and acquaintances to think of me not primarily as an invalid but as a neighbor and friend, and to treat me the same way.

Besides make-up and nicely-scented toilet articles, I like attractive bed-wear. All these are morale builders. During my first years in the hospital, my wardrobe was mainly plaster of Paris casts, bulky gowns, and well-bleached sheets. Later I graduated into braces attached to clumsy shoes, pastel blouses, bed-jackets, and more sheets. Then one Christmas a cousin gave me a shirt so bright that I could be seen a corridor away. A new era had begun.

In 1946 the next innovation was a lap robe made of seersucker. It was pretty, but it was lined with crepe and so slippery it wouldn't stay in place. "You'll have to do better than that," my mother said. I tried, but the next one — made of drapery material — had all the charm and coolness of a horse blanket.

Corduroy entered my life soon afterward with matching slippers adding another dash of color below my robes. Today a new material — sailcloth — makes the most practical and inexpensive coverlets of all. They are washable and wrinkle-resistant, and they suit my purpose, taste, and pocketbook. My blouses hit a jackpot of color. I have them in checks, polka dots, plaids and stripes, and in a wide variety of materials. My mother's favorites, needless to say, are blouses made of the wrinkle-proof, drip-dry fabrics that require little or no ironing.

Once on a pilgrimage a co-traveler exclaimed over my abundance of blouses as though I had invested a small fortune in them. Amused at the thought, I explained that even my best ones cost no more than three or four dollars, since less than two yards of material is needed for one blouse.

"But it surely takes more than that with long full sleeves?"

"Not for me," I replied. "Since I don't lift my arms, the sleeves don't need any extra shoulder action and because my arms don't straighten, my sleeve length is short."

"But there's still a collar and a good-sized piece for the back and — "

I laughed. "Around my neck is merely a narrow strap, and in the back there are only two panels just wide enough to fasten onto the sleeves. . . ."

"You mean there's no real back in your blouse? But how in the world do they stay on?" my inquisitor asked, her eyes opened wide.

"My dear, the answer to that is one of the advantages of immobility."

Another advantage is the fun of owning a brand new aluminum ambulance cot. It can be elevated to the height of a hospital bed in three seconds. No stoop. No squat. No strain. While my lifters shout its praises, I lie quietly on my precarious perch and pray I won't fall off.

The invoice arrived from the undertakers' supply house, where the cot was purchased, with a page illustrating other items of merchandise. As Mother held it up for me to see, I gasped, "Oh, gee! Just what I've always wanted!" She turned curious eyes toward the page. "May the Lord bless us!" she sputtered. "Embalming tables!"

To parents and friends of the sick and disabled who are bounded by four walls, I am eager to pass along some suggestions that have enriched my life. They are not all original; nor do I expect them to be unanimously approved. Most invalids seem to have their own devices — ones which are acquired with much planning and ingenuity — so it is with humility that I submit my hints. Compared to many, my bedfast years may seem as a drop in the bucket and my tips no hotter than yesterday's mashed potatoes.

Brightening the sickroom is a must that can be achieved inexpensively and easily. Get away from "bedroomy" curtains. Use gay multicolored drapes and matching spreads to give the carefree air of a studio. The effect can be carried out in skirts for the dressing table and bench and covers for radiators. Washable materials can be kept fresh through laundering, with an alternate ensemble for an occasional change of atmosphere as well as the scenery.

Brightly decorated serving trays and cloths, dishes, salt and pepper shakers, glasses and napkins also add a splash of color. If my mother serves me only cold meat, potato chips, hard-boiled eggs, a peach, and a glass of milk, she presents it so attractively that it's like dining in a swanky hotel.

For that rare item, steak, we make use of another gift — a small electric hot plate which keeps the meat sizzling while my rheumatic jaws go slowly about their business. During the lemonade season Mother places a pint pitcher on my tray to save her refill trips to the kitchen. If my capacity exceeds the prescribed pint, I am told firmly, "Sorry, Susie Q., but I intend to sleep tonight!"

Scrapbook enthusiasts know the problem it is to store these ungainly volumes in the space usually allotted to them by drawers and closets. I finally coaxed a neighbor into building a large open book case with a deep cupboard underneath to house all my souvenirs, year books, and other treasured flotsam. The book case, however, is only a temporary solution. My mother summed it up just the other day after three attempts to close the lower doors. "Something's gotta give. . . ."

Simplifying personal care and comfort are such trusty aids as a "Kelly Pad"—a round rubber pad used to shampoo a patient's hair (the outer edge is inflated in a C form, and a flat piece extends out and down into a pail); an inflatable back rest whose portability makes "has been" lumpy pillows out of date; rubber thumb stalls which, when filled with cold cream, soften up hard-to-trim fingernails; and foam rubber by the yard. For this last miracle, I earnestly thank God. Pieces of it support my head and heels, cushion my feet and elbows, and elevate my legs to the desired height—and without lumps. I sit on a foam rubber cushion, lie on a foam rubber mattress when I'm on my cot and, sometimes while day dreaming, I float through space on a foam rubber cloud. A pink one.

Some helpful gadgets which I recommend: metal reading stands, a commercial timer that turns the television or radio on and off, an overhead arrangement of canvas straps and pulleys for lifting a heavy or immobile patient, an intercom set for one who is alone a great deal and likes to share in kitchen conversation, and a hard rubber clamp-like device that holds a telephone receiver for those who cannot.

My dictaphone and writing stand make my working hours easier. The latter was originally an adjustable serving and reading stand, remodeled to suit my needs. On this we clamp letters, copy to proofread, or a manuscript to be revised. If I could use my hands other than to write, I'd have liked two shallow side drawers for a ready supply of stationery. As it is, when I run out of ammunition, Mother—bless her—is usually within call.

Gifts for the chronically ill pose a serious problem, so friends tell me. Patients, on the other hand, lament a surfeit of potted African

Violets, soap, bath salts, joke books, and bed jackets. It isn't that they aren't appreciated, but there are so many other things we would rather have. So for the sake of shut-ins and those who are bewildered as to selection, here are a few items that are guaranteed morale boosters for the disabled: novelty earrings, bracelets, and other costume jewelry, bed lamp, hair dryer, phonograph records, ceramic figurines, unusual vases, beverage glasses, ash trays (invalids frequently play the role of a host or hostess, you know), serving trays, colored bed linen, plastic carry-alls, fitted overnight bag, billfold, clutch bag, jewel box, letter file, portable strong box, a picture that blends in with the patient's room, an individual carafe set, a magazine subscription, camera, electric fan, blessed candles, desk cloth, the Stations of the Cross, a miniature shrine, hanging ivy plant, parakeet (only with permission of the one who will be taking care of it!), photo album, cuff links, books (if one knows the patient's reading tastes), games, and the various supplements for hobbies.

Such are the externals that comprise the life of an invalid. Some of them simplify it, others complicate it. Some awaken interest and ambition, others awaken only memories of healthier days. Some create joy, others restlessness. It is important for a shut-in to distinguish the things that help from those that hinder. As a busy paraplegic veteran once told me, "My life changed the day I chose to read a booklet on engraving instead of one on racket-busting."

"Take the nice things that come to you, Mary Ellen," a priest once advised, "and be both grateful and glad for them. But lest their worth be magnified, remember that they have value only so long as they do not interfere with God's plan for you."

I often think of those priestly words when a nice gift arrives — probably because at such moments my unworthiness is always showing. I am grateful for the lovely trimmings of my life and wonder sometimes if, like the lonely and forgotten in drab county homes and hospitals, I shall ever be stripped of them. Should it happen to me in the years to come, one thing is certain: I'll hold fast to my lipstick.

CHAPTER 11

HAVE COT—WILL TRAVEL

A SOFT August rain was falling when we arrived at the depot, and the mugginess made my mattress feel like a steam oven. A ten block "stroll" in the rain the evening before had left me with a stuffed-up head. Only the prospect of our destination lifted my spirit.

I was on my way at last to meet Father Boyd, an arthritic priest with whom I had corresponded for years. Ever since his walking days ended in 1930, he had resided at St. John's Hospital in Rapid City, South Dakota. Meeting him now after becoming friends through letters would be like seeing a person materialize out of a dream.

This trip had all the earmarks of adventure for another reason too — it was being made in a baggage car!

Few girls besides Helen Kovarna would have undertaken a thousand-mile trip with me in such noisy, dirty quarters which we shared with an unhappy cocker spaniel. Our accommodations were roomy enough, but the acoustics could scarcely be recommended. We shouted at each other until my voice played out. Able neither to hear nor make signals, I had to communicate with Kovarna through an exaggerated lip reading, a process complicated by my nose, which she had to wipe constantly.

"How would you two like the doors open?" the baggageman asked solicitously. "You can see the Bad Lands better that way."

"By all means!" we replied. "Both doors." It meant looking at *something* beside baggagecar walls, even though it meant another layer of dirt.

Through one wide opening and then the other we stared at the tomb-like spires that resembled a graveyard. There was no movement except for the drifting surface sand, and any sound that might have been heard was drowned out by the train as it hurtled across the prairie. We watched the sun descend behind the ghostly mounds. Soon the gray gauze of twilight wrapped itself around them like a shroud and in a few moments they disappeared in the oblivion of darkness.

"It won't be long now," the baggageman announced after twelve hours of travel. Kovarna tried to wash my face, but by the time she staggered to the rest room three cars ahead, and staggered back, little water remained in the paper cup. Dirt removing with granulated soap and crumbly paper towels was a notable fiasco. But after all, we reminded each other, both Rapid City and hot, soapy water were just around the corner.

The hospital was dark and silent when we arrived at Father Boyd's room. We said good night to the ambulance drivers; then Kovarna knocked softly on the door. I was surprised to hear a deep, resonant "Come!" Eight years of arthritis had weakened my voice; after seventeen years with the same disease, Father's sounded like a trumpet. Kovarna pushed my cot into the room and turned it around.

There before me in an overstuffed armchair sat the priest I had come to see. White hair spoke of age, hunched shoulders of pain, blanket-covered feet of long confinement. His piercing blue eyes caught and held my attention. Suddenly, these marks of suffering faded into a background dominated by the eyes of a man whose ability and influence had refused to be tethered.

Father welcomed us warmly, and as I heard his voice, he emerged gradually into the person with whom I had long corresponded. I sensed the qualities that gave to his letters a depth and stimulation I had found in no others. A man of great perception and subtle wit, he seemed to feel out his guests in a way that was as revealing as it was inoffensive — and by no means was it an uncomfortable he-can-see-right-through-me feeling. In less than twenty minutes, I felt that he knew me almost as well as if we had met a hundred times. In a way, I was relieved: I wanted him to know me, and our time was too short to waste it on surface chitchat.

"If I could remain here under Father's tutelage," I told Kovarna after our first day in Rapid City, "I might still amount to something!" He had the great gift of imparting to others his knowledge and wisdom, a gift no doubt developed while instructing the nurses in sociology, psychology, and psychiatry. He has an innate sense of the dramatic which compliments his vibrant voice. He rivaled Barrymore himself — especially in reading aloud Francis Thompson's "Hound of Heaven."

A man of his purpose and sensitivity must have suffered intensely when, at 30, arthritis ended his duties at the Cathedral. All attempts to recover failed; soon he was permanently disabled, except for partial use of his hands and arms. But he taught student nurses, instructed prospective converts, and gave freely of his time and help to all in need of advice. The number has increased each year, for the clergy as well as the laity turned to him.

To many he is but a voice. During the war years he was asked to narrate from his hospital room a Christmas Eve Mass to be broadcast at midnight from the city's Cathedral. Unknowingly he set a precedent still observed. The technical aspects of this task were nerve-racking. But even harder to bear must have been the memory of having once stood in the sanctuary where the ceremony was now being carried on.

But whatever the cost to himself, he did the job, and handsomely. A pilot wrote him that he had listened to the broadcast in his plane and that it had jolted him into remembering his boyhood faith. As soon as he returned to his base, he went to the chapel and made his peace with God.

Each day I saw something different in Father Boyd. One moment he was a towering giant, the next a merry leprechaun with a light in his eyes and a lilt in his voice. One day, when a lock of hair fell on his forehead, he even reminded me of Peter Pan.

Since 1930 he had left his room only three times. I understood why he refused to venture out for occasionally I too had feared leaving my room, or, to be more exact, returning to it. But because his reluctance was more deeply rooted than mine, he regarded departure from his wall-to-wall security as a threat to the years he spent in adjusting to confinement. To him, no promised pleasure justified the risk of having to rebuild another lonely, isolated world.

Regardless of his personal feelings, he wanted his guests to see all they could. Thanks to Father and a local mortician, Kovarna and I were shown most of the sights which draw so many tourists to the Black Hills. Our favorite was Mount Rushmore, on which the faces of four presidents are ingeniously carved. As two young embalmers carried me up a narrow path for a better view, I looked into the sky and prayed silently, "Dear God, thank You for creating undertakers!"

In 1941, in honor of Father Boyd's silver jubilee, the priests of the Rapid City Diocese obtained from Rome the permission for him to offer Mass while seated. Because of this greatly desired dispensation, I was privileged to attend his Masses during my visit. On the last morning Kovarna, though not of my faith, stayed with me for a very special reason. When I learned that Father hadn't given Holy Communion to anyone for sixteen years, I quickly judged the distance from the lap table (which also serves as his altar) to my cot. With a little crowding, it would seem that he could reach me. After I mentioned it to him, his eagerness to try filled me with an uneasiness that lasted all night.

With exquisite reverence, Father began the familiar "In nomine Patris, et Filii, et Spiritus Sancti." The prayers of the Holy Sacrifice struck me as never before — perhaps because I had never witnessed its enactment so closely. This was the extension of Calvary . . . the rebirth of the Sacramental Christ . . . the apex of my life. I looked at the celebrant and thought with a start: *How truly is he a priest!* His altar — a wood table, his pulpit — an armchair, his parish — the unseen audience of his Sunday radio broadcasts. And yet as he lifted the gold paten with crippled hands, neither a cathedral nor splendid vestments nor a mighty choir could have enhanced the majesty of the starkly beautiful drama taking place before me.

On that paten I mentally placed my hopes, gratitude, contrition and love, and asked God to bless that devout victim, that "Other Christ."

The Communion bell sounded the warning that the moment had arrived. The nun answering the responses looked at me and nodded. To Kovarna I whispered, "Now," and as she brought my cot close to the table altar, I strained forward to receive the Host held in the crippled, trembling fingers of the afflicted priest. . . . In the wordless moment that followed, two human crosses became as one with the cross of Calvary — here renewed eucharistically.

Before 1950 arrived, I had logged another eighty-three hundred miles. The majority of them I covered on a train, the rest in a milk truck, laundry delivery wagon, a panel owned by a painter, de-seated autos, a pickup truck, station wagon, and by no means least, Perassos' hearse. While visiting some of my favorite relatives in Dubuque, another mode of travel appeared. I was on my way to the Trappist Monastery with Bernie Chicoine and several seminarians (all former Trinity friends) when the tie rod in Bernie's panel truck went out. No one panicked but in view of the slope of the hill we were on, I'm sure we all prayed furiously as we ended halfway in a ditch. Carefully the boys lifted my cot from the truck, a process delayed by the temporary disappearance of our pliers — a major item since the handle on the panel's back door had come off several weeks earlier. At that moment a bewhiskered Trappist monk came along beside us in an empty hay wagon. Politely but with obvious surprise at seeing me, he told us to "come aboard." For the rest of the ride to the New Melleray Abbey, I viewed the Dubuque hills — those my mother so dearly loved — from a lofty perch.

After Dubuque came Denver, thanks to an invitation from that blue-eyed maverick, Mary Jackman, and her lawyer-to-be husband, Bob Burns. This was my first time with Jackman since our trip to Canada in 1948, and though we could keep ourselves amused indefinitely, she and Bob showed me Denver from parks to skid row; cool green Estes Park; and Central City, with its famous Teller

House, the site of the "Face on the Barroom Floor." I was glad I had taken Horace Greeley's advice.

With Jackman as my companion, the trip home would have been enjoyable except for one thing — our return was made in the baggage car, where the heat exceeded the 90 degree temperature outside.

* * * * * *

"I'll be present when you are ordained. That's a promise."

I had made this solemn promise to the first LaSalette Brothers I met at Lake Okoboji, and for five years I prayed that the promise could be kept. Thanks to Our Lady of La Salette, it was.

On a sunny May afternoon a gray ambulance turned off Topsfield Road, near Ipswich, Massachusetts, into a winding, tree-canopied driveway that led to the LaSalette Seminary. The confusion of Boston, thirty miles away, seemed remote as we passed through a high iron gate and stopped before a graceful statue of our Lady. Nearby, a Japanese cherry tree stood in strange contrast to its sturdy cousins and curtsied daintily with its billowy pink frock. Beyond, as far as I could see, were trees.

The Seminary, the former home of a shipping magnate, because of its authentic resemblance to an English manor, had once been used for scenes in the motion picture "13 Rue Madeleine." Here and there on the mansion's red brick walls, lettuce-green ivy scrambled toward the roof top where a slender cross looked down on all below.

The structure housing these men was basically elegant, obviously built by wealth for people of wealth. And the LaSalettes were bound voluntarily to a life of poverty. Their sacrifices and accomplishments, their peace and contentment, impressed me more than all the paneled walls and fireplaces put together.

Ann Marten, my intelligent and humorous companion from near Chicago, and I stayed in the guest house at night. In the mornings we wakened to a symphony, with bluejays ably handling the rhythm section, goldfinches on the strings, two talented orioles as first and second flutists, and an itinerant woodpecker on the drums. No wonder they had inspired Edgar Fawcett to write:

"At some glad moment was it Nature's choice
To dower a scrap of sunset with a voice?"

These birds witnessed a strange sight one morning during our visit. Ann had assembled the wood in the fireplace, made a fire, and set a pan of water on to heat for bathing me. But the logs crumbled to ashes and the water splashed in all directions. I had to bathe in cold water, and not even the musical background made it pleasant.

Ann went upstairs to brush her teeth. "I'll be back in a jiffy," she said, "and finish dressing." Less than five minutes later, a gust of wind banged the door shut. Soon I heard Ann knocking on the other side.

"Hey! What happened?" she called through the door.

"It was the wind. Can't you open the door?"

"No."

At first I thought she was clowning. Then I noticed the Yale lock. I called. "It looks as though you are locked out."

For several minutes even the birds were silent. And then they heard a noise at the window. "Oh, Lord, no!" I cried, my stomach shaking with laughter. For there in her pajamas and robe, her hair up in pin curls and a toothbrush clenched in her hand, was Ann, climbing laboriously in through the window!

The sun shone bright on the day of ordinations. Years of careful preparation had ended; now the four deacons soon would be ready to harvest the fruits of their study. I watched episcopal hands administer to them the sacrament of Holy Orders. The power and responsibility being invested in them hit me with a tremendous impact.

To the families of these young men, these scenes undoubtedly stirred memories of their boyhood; to the Brothers still preparing, a glowing inspiration; and to the priest instructors, the sweet remembrance of a similar day when, prostrate before an equally beautiful altar, they pledged themselves to the service of God until death and into Eternity. To me it brought that fusion of joy and sadness that tightens the throat and swells the heart.

In the refectory that evening, the Brothers joined the new priests in presenting a music fest for the two midwestern guests. Aided by a violin, clarinet, and guitar, they sang the praises of the Rose of Tralee, Mother Machree, and Moriarity the Cop. They tunefully described the conditions at Birmingham Jail, conjured up a scene of Moonlight and Roses, and took Kathleen home at least three times.

The ten o'clock bell reminded us that all good things must end. Following us through the foyer, the Brothers filed out through the wide door at the front of the house and remained standing there as my cot was being pushed past the statue and on toward the gate. I had just asked to be turned to face them when the paraphrased lyrics of a familiar tune burst into the inky darkness, and until we rounded the bend I heard them singing, "Good night, good night . . . we'll see you in the morning. . . ."

The next day one of the Brothers informed Ann and me that a tour through the grounds "is a must."

Over acres of landscaped terraces I was alternately pushed and carried. The first level, which overlooked the pool and the front lawn like a balcony, was partly encircled by a low stone railing and trimmed hedges.

A flight of brick steps took us to a second level where apple, cherry, and pear trees proudly stood their ground. In the center, almost hidden by an overhead trellis, was a wishing well. I had no coin to toss in, but it did not matter — I had nothing to wish for.

When we reached the next level I exclaimed in amazement, "Now I've seen everything!" Rising up from a concrete base was a *bird* cage ten feet high and six feet wide! No feathered prisoners were in this wire bastille, but once its cocky occupants had preened themselves before amused guests. "What do you think of it, Mary Ellen?" one of the Brothers asked.

I couldn't help myself. "It's for the birds, all right."

The tour was climaxed with a "special treat" — Ipswich fried clams. That night I returned with Ann to the cottage and watched the embers die. After she fell asleep, I concluded that it was a good thing for me happiness wasn't charged up to a person like a grocery bill. I decided then to go to sleep, but I didn't. Too many clams.

Our last day at the Seminary went so fast that it frightened me and dulled my appetite. I even declined homemade pizza brought from Brooklyn by the parents of one of the Brothers. Because of Boston's heavy traffic, good-bys had to be cut short. When the time came for leaving, Ann and I went silently with our black-cassocked hosts to the entrance where the gray ambulance waited. Lifted in backward, I was dismayed when I saw that the rear door barred my vision, shutting out everything but the road beside the ambulance. But it was too late to do anything about it.

As we drove away, all I could see was an array of black shoes that stood there without moving until they were finally swallowed up as we passed through the gate for the last time.

A promise had been kept: a dream had come true.

CHAPTER 12

SO LONG, MIKE

THE New Year, 1949, was around several days before we were aware of its presence. My father had been very ill, and since the day after Thanksgiving we had measured time, not in the usual day-and-night sequence, but only as an hourly extension of life for Dad.

Disregarding her own ill health (four days earlier she had been dismissed from a nearby hospital) Mom boarded the train in the cold darkness of that holiday evening and set out for Iowa City, where my father was a patient at the University Hospital. On the following morning she received the verdict: an inoperable malignancy.

"How — how long will he have, Doctor?" she asked.

"That is only for God to say, Mrs. Kelly. All we can do is make a very human estimate — "

"And your estimate . . . ?"

"Possibly three months. Maybe five . . . "

On the eighth day of December, the feast of our Lady's Immaculate Conception, Dad came home. As soon as he was resting comfortably in the downstairs bedroom about twenty feet from the living room corner occupied by my bed, he called to me:

"Hi there, old-timer! How are you?"

"Hi, Mike!" I called back. "We're so terribly glad you're home!"

"I'm sorry I didn't get in to see you before they landed me in bed," he added, referring to the ambulance attendants, "but I will after a little while . . . , well — maybe not today — but tomorrow for sure!"

I couldn't answer. I knew that this was one promise he wouldn't be able to keep.

God was good. Dad grew weaker each day, but he was spared the pain that we feared would be his. We were grateful for this, although his increasing weakness was hard to accept. Both Mom's and Dad's attitude throughout these weeks made a lasting impression on me. Mother assumed the care of her new patient as cheerfully as a woman dons a new dress. Overnight her duties doubled, but she complained to no one, asked for no help, and never caused either Dad or me to feel that we were a burden.

My father had always been a patient man. Now he drew deeply of this virtue from the storehouse which practice had richly stocked. If he knew that death was imminent, he gave no sign; nor did he and Mother discuss it in any way until the evening he was anointed. He took her hand in his and whispered hoarsely, "I guess this is it, Bridgie." With that same economy of words afforded by love, Mother pressed her face again his and answered simply, "Yes, darling, I guess it is."

Four days later, just at sundown, their thirty-five years of marriage came to an end. The hours that followed are hazy in my memory, though I remember clearly the last moments of that unhappy day.

Mother declined the offer of relatives to stay with us overnight. She quietly lowered my backrest, elevated my feet and covered me with my blanket. We talked over the men we would ask to be pallbearers, and discussed other details which neither of us had wanted to mention while Dad still lived. My brother would not be arriving until the next evening, so I tried to conceal my sorrow so as to comfort her all I could, for surely her grief was greater than mine. My intentions were good, but I had little opportunity to put them into effect. For in the quiet, capable way that she performed the duties still to be done, I realized that Someone else was supplying her with courage and comfort.

Hearing Casey on my window sill, Mother let him in and gave him a saucer of milk. She locked the doors, wound the clock and put Casey in the basement. Suddenly a great weariness seemed to envelop her. With visible effort she wheeled my ambulance cot to a spot halfway between my room and Dad's and, as she had done for sixty-three consecutive nights, lay down on the improvised bed from which she had been able to hear a call from either room. That night her sleep was not disturbed.

Life went on. Faced with a column deadline four days later, I decided on a letter to Dad himself, in which I wrote in part:

You have been gone for several days; yet it is impossible to believe that you are gone forever. Your favorite chair, your ashtray, glasses, overcoat — all your things have a waiting look . . . and a lost look too, as though aware that their usefulness is over.

As a friend wrote in a letter that came this morning: "Something loved is never lost; you loved Mike, so you will always have Mike." That is surely the way it is, Dad, for just as I am part of you, so are you part of me . . .

Though you had no particular talent, how your quiet humor made me laugh! Your household skill was limited to replacing a fuse, putting on storm windows, and washing dishes. But whatever you did you did well and with no complaint. . . . I'm glad we were such good friends, Dad, and our tastes so alike (especially when it came to Mom's chicken gravy).

. . . In trying now to list the reasons why my heart is overflowing with gratitude, I must say THANKS for my first real-haired doll, clock and suitcase . . . the coat with the beaver collar . . . for all the popcorn you fed me. Thanks, too, for your tears, heartaches, your forgiveness when I disappointed you . . . for the comfort you gave me, your encouragement, the example of patience you set for me. . . . Thanks for the way you always looked at me — as though I were something special — and for the gentle way you spoke my name. . . .

CHAPTER 13

THIS MATTER OF SOLITUDE

WHY are people so afraid of being alone? Why does a hospital patient beg guests to stay longer? Why does a person chew his nails, drum his fingers, or pace about the room if he has to be by himself for half an hour?

Because the society we live in has turned us into clock punchers, commuters, dawn-to-dark-working farmers, swing-shift mechanics, two-job firemen, and get-ahead-or-else executives. If we don't drive a big car, live in a fancy house, we're considered peasants, or, at best, nonconformists.

So we establish the rapid pace necessary to keep us on top. Once it's a habit, we regard a quiet moment with horror. The minute there's a lull, boredom creeps in, nerves get jumpy, restlessness takes over. Nearly everyone faces these disconnected moments sooner or later and rallies from them. But what about men and women who are abruptly snatched from this swift pace and plunged into a long succession of solitary moments? What happens to these victims of an accident or disabling illness?

For a few days there is such a concentration of activity about the new patient that he longs for some privacy. Finally his wish is granted. He is alone. Solitude in this get-acquainted period is like a big black bird that silently waits to pounce upon him the minute the door closes behind his last guest.

I remember these first encounters with aloneness almost too clearly for comfort. Time suddenly conspires to overthrow sanity and undermine defenses. Nighttime is the worst. Pain, loneliness, the sounds of the hospital, the day's disappointments, your problems — even the shadows on the wall are exaggerated. Panic starts in your stomach, then uncurls like an octopus that keeps reaching into every part of you. For the first time you are alone — a chilling, stark, silent aloneness — and your heart shrinks into a corner as fear moves in. I know. It happened to me.

My change from normal activity wasn't as dramatic as it is with many others. I had been ill for weeks; yet overnight my way of life was changed. Soon I faced the same problem as one who had been switched from far greater activity: how to decrease speed, yet keep one's battery sufficiently charged to travel the rough roads ahead?

Because the answer to that question is extremely important, I would like to recall the process step by step as I remember it. If my telling helps even one chronic invalid adjust to and understand the potential of solitude, I won't regret the pain of remembrance.

At the outset of your new role, pain usually prevents you from calm reasoning. You live one hour at a time, afraid to look ahead, and not wanting to look back, held in the vise of the tormenting present. Food holds no interest; thirst nags at you as relentlessly as pain.

When it abates, you gradually realize you are no longer the same. Now you are a patient. You have other new titles too: an arthritic, a paraplegic, an amputee. Fruits, flowers, and get-well cards come less often. So do visitors. One morning you know THIS IS IT. This is no appendectomy honeymoon, no week-end tonsilectomy. This is "for real."

Until this time, solitude to me was only as a word used in convents, torch songs, and stories about the Foreign Legion. Now as a patient, it was a vacuum, a dull interlude between visitors, an enforced rest period. In my early moments of aloneness I often sang to myself or daydreamed. There was nothing I could do with my hands so I prayed, counted cracks in the ceiling, wondered what I'd do with a million dollars, pretended I was at home cleaning dresser drawers, or traveling around the world.

The days dragged on. I tired of counting cracks, taking imaginary trips and singing to myself. Even daydreams lost their appeal. I couldn't move, but neither could I bear to lie there day in and day out and wither with boredom.

This was the turning point, the spiritual and psychological fork in the road. When I paused to choose my direction I realized two important things: first, in God's plan my illness was no accident. He permitted this to happen to me from all eternity. Second, God couldn't possibly have given me the wrong cross. This is the one with my measurements, my name. This one alone would be my key to heaven; none other would open the gates. I reached these conclusions with our Lady's help, and her guidance headed me in the right direction.

Then one day I felt a peculiar excitement and expectation. It seemed as though I were waiting for someone or something. Sometimes I even heard a faint, insistent voice (conscience?) whisper: "Make use of your solitude." As though afraid that obeying the voice would involve me too deeply, I pretended not to hear.

But not always. I heeded the small voice a few times and glimpsed at last the unique and beautiful world to which prayerful solitude leads. Once this happened, my soul became a restless thing torn between the desire to return to that world and the near annihilation of self that the trip requires. For certain rules are necessary in order to proceed, and what rule ever escaped rebellion? A simple one like establishing a set time for interior recollection is the one I break most frequently. One day my excuse is tiredness, the next pain. Then my heart reaches for something that is out of bounds. Effort is made to begin the journey again, but this unlawful possession weighs me down. I make attempts to bypass this spiritual roadblock, but I can't. Since it can't be avoided or ignored, and since I often lack the courage to remove it, I resort to the easiest alternative of all: postponing the whole thing.

That's how it has been with solitude and me through the years — a fight for it, a fight against it. I've learned this about solitude: it is vital to spiritual advancement, and its wonders are not revealed at once, but slowly, cautiously, in keeping with one's capacity to understand them. I also learned that asking direction from the Mother of God is wise. Perhaps others may not feel as reluctant as I to go ahead without her; but I see in Mary the ideal example of the fruits of solitude. For nine months she was alone with Christ, united in the most intimate of all human relationships. After His birth she remained the same blessed temple, no longer the literal vessel of Incarnate Love, but one filled to capacity with His grace. She is, as St. Louis de Montfort said, ". . . the admirable Mother of the Son . . . the sealed fountain and faithful spouse of the Holy Ghost . . . and the sanctuary and blessed repose of the Blessed Trinity."

Now the big question: What exactly, does one do in these periods of solitude? What is the goal? I should like to repeat that the answers I have found are personal ones, and that if to some they seem unorthodox, impotent, or foolish, I am not making a defense.

First of all, I regard these periods apart from the daily prayer time all Christians should observe. That is what you might call an extracurricular activity for establishing a better relationship between teacher and student, rather than to afford the latter additional credit hours.

My first step is acknowledging my unworthiness before God and begging His forgiveness for all my sins, for the good I overlooked and could have done better, for not loving Him enough, and for offering contrition streaked with selfishness of one kind or another. Next I take a quick inventory of the endless things He has given me: sight, hearing, taste, speech, a home, family, a kind pastor, friends, books, music, God's supernatural gifts, and all the other things that add joy to my life.

Then I simply try to relax, blotting out as many as possible of the sounds and objects about me, as though shutting the door on the world. I ask Mary to help me empty my mind, heart, and soul of all distractions so that nothing will block the way in case God chooses to send me some graces. . . . Then comes an invitation to the Holy Ghost to be present at the meeting soon to take place. The words vary from time to time, but usually go something like this:

"*O divine Spirit of Love, on the other side of this moment is the time of union between Christ and me. I ask You to accompany* me to this meeting and remain throughout so that my heart will be a lovely trysting place.

"Give me the ability to love, contemplate, trust, praise, and thank my Saviour as never before. Increase my appreciation of His beauty, my understanding of my own unworthiness, and my determination to offend Him no more. This I ask in His Holy Name, which the angels glorify throughout eternity."

Later, reaching out for our Lady's hand, I ask:

"Come, stand beside me, sweet Virgin Mother! Cleanse my soul with but a touch of your loveliness and fill it with at least some measure of your tenderness. Only if you do this can I hope to build a worthy resting place for Him who redeemed me. Teach me how to derive the utmost from this solitude which, through illness, is now mine. Grant, dear Mother, that I will neither waste nor reject it, but instead will co-operate to the fullest with the opportunities it affords. Obtain charity for me so that my lips may speak words of love . . . patience so that I will not be disappointed when my efforts produce only a seeming emptiness . . . purity to behold God . . . and courage so that my solitude will never degenerate into rebellion or self-pity.

"Impress on me the value of withdrawing from the worthless interests and habits that clutter up my soul and leave so little room for Christ. Thus far I am able only to put a small amount of my solitude to good use, but with your help maybe I can even come to love such moments and seek them deliberately. And before Your Son and I meet at last, tell Him that in spite of my repeated offenses, I really do love Him. From You, sweet Comforter of the Afflicted, I confidently seek these favors. Amen."

And the meeting itself? How can I describe it when it is never the same way twice? How can I evaluate something that may be disappointing the very time I put forth the most effort, and beautiful when I am most unworthy? Frankly, I don't think I can, but maybe these thoughts will serve as a substitute.

When God made the world and created human beings to live in it, I believe that He decided to write a symphony for each and every person, with no two alike, yet each a masterpiece. And so when a person loves God and obeys His will, heaven resounds with the music resulting from that soul's symphony. When personal desires are given priority, a discord strikes a mournful tone. As the Divine Composer, He could easily demand that each soul play a perfect score; however, He does not desire a mechanical, heartless rendition, but rather music that flows from love and sacrifice. In this way, each symphony retains its individual theme and is free to add to its personal variations.

The more a soul loves God, the sweeter is the music flowing from its meeting with Him. At times the heart and mind are so joyously in tune with His that breathing itself becomes a gentle rhythm that contributes, like one's pounding pulse, to a well-directed musical production.

During these moments it is difficult to determine what is responsible for such a beautiful blend. Is it the integrity of the performer? — Or the love and generosity of the Divine Maestro? — Or both?

I know there will be other meetings, which will produce no music — at least not that my heart can hear. When one of these occurs, my pulse will pound in monotonous cadence as breaths follow one another like weary sighs. Then from somewhere within I will hear the refrain of a familiar rhapsody; yet no amount of effort will release the melody, no amount of longing will set free the taunting notes. Rather it is better to let the melody flow freely over oneself like gentle waves, even though such surrender requires an enormous act of humility and trust.

But who knows? Perhaps in God's ear each individual symphony is performed more perfectly during these moments of seeming silence than at any other time. Whether they are or not doesn't concern me too much. I know that the important thing is to try to make use of each moment of each day, trusting that God will decide which ones please Him most and bear the greatest merit. For only with relentless perseverance and effort can the heart hope to resist all that might destroy or even intrude upon the spiritual temple slowly built by prayerful and dedicated solitude.

In the words of Thomas à Kempis:

"In silence and quiet the devout soul advances in virtue and learns the hidden truths of Scripture. There she finds a flood of tears with which to bathe and cleanse herself nightly, that she may become the more intimate with her Creator the farther she withdraws from all the tumult of the world. For God and His holy angels will draw near to him who withdraws from friends and acquaintances."*

* *The Imitation of Christ* by Thomas à Kempis (Milwaukee: The Bruce Publishing Co.), Book One, Chapter 20.

CHAPTER 14

WESTWARD HO!

DURING my years as a hospital patient I became an expert at day-dreaming. My daydreaming was at night before going to sleep. Then, my favored dream pictured me at home where I was busily engaged in (of all things) housecleaning!

From room to room I waged a battle against dust, and when the time came for the window-washing sequence I merely accelerated the pace like an actor in those first flickering movies, and went on to rearranging furniture, cleaning dresser and cabinet drawers, and repainting the kitchen chairs. A devotee of Freud might read deep inner disturbances into this recurrent dream pattern but it afforded me more pleasure than any imaginary romance with some tall, dark, mysterious stranger.

But after I returned home, this pastime understandably lost its appeal. As a substitute, I often made a mental list of my friendships during my hospitalization. Depression was always dispelled as I remembered the kindness of those on the list, and this backward glance showed me that illness had its compensations.

But one summer day in 1951 my mental inventory left me with a new sensation — the feeling of standing still while all my friends were whizzing by. Kovarna and Kennedy were married. . . . "High-pockets" had two handsome black-eyed sons . . . Steve and Helen's Mike was almost six . . . Jim, Roger, and Leon had returned from Army duty overseas and soon would enter their third year in college . . . Mabel (as pretty as ever) and Paul were the parents of two little girls, the miniature of their mother . . . and the fellows I had known at Trinity College, whose doors were now closed, were scattered all over the country.

In the middle of my reminiscing, a visitor arrived with an astonishing invitation. Her name was Alma and to Mother and me she declared that we were to go to California for four weeks as her guests! No dose of vitamins could have more quickly restored the bloom to my cheeks.

The excitement of our preparation was added to by a telegram from Andy Kelly, a cousin in Los Angeles. We had never met, but I knew from the family grapevine that this former Chicagoan was in the advertising business; that he had his own weekly television program called "Fishin's Fun"; and that his charm and gift of gab were terrific.

I wrote Andy of our coming and asked if he could arrange for me to see Catalina and attend a Groucho Marx program. He replied by wire:

> All set. Proper transportation everywhere duration your stay. Radio and television shows. Studio visits. Cruise on Pacific et cetera. Full "Red Rug" treatment. Have chatted with Alma. My letter follows in a few days.
>
> Love
> Andy

The Leo Carillo television show was my introduction to Hollywood. Placed next to the camera on the runway, I was briefed on such terms as "boom-mike," "dummy sheets," "fadeouts," and "split screens." It seemed odd to be learning the technical lingo when all I had seen of TV itself was one snowy wrestling match. But it was part of the fun and I enjoyed every minute of it.

The proverbial charm of the Hollywood male was upheld admirably by the show's star, Leo Carillo. Doffing his white ten-gallon hat he kissed me soundly when we met and twice at leaving. This gesture, though a little surprising, was merely an expression of friendliness and accepted as such. Yet, I smiled at the thought of Marcus men adopting a similar salutation.

With the wheels removed from my cot, I fitted comfortably into Andy's Kaiser "Traveler"; however, as the cot was too long for the upper half of the rear opening to be closed, my head was outside. In this "open air taxi" I was shown the places I had read and heard about since childhood: the Brown Derby; Grauman's Chinese Theatre; the Cocoanut Grove; Olvera Street; the mysterious avenues of Chinatown; Sunset Boulevard, and the shores of the blue Pacific, where snow-white sea gulls executed intricate maneuvers for the price of a bread crust.

When we were not on the road, I gave my undivided attention to the television set Andy rented for us during the weeks of our visit. There were only a few coast to coast shows at that time, but to me it made no difference. The Congressional investigation of alleged subversive activities among Hollywood writers was more suspenseful than scripts from "Inner Sanctum." Sharing my liking for the Lawrence Welk show but not television in general, Alma looked from the inviting patio to me (who found even the commercials interesting) and sighed, "Don't you want to get out in the sun, Mary Ellen?"

John Knapp, my good friend from hospital days, had worked in California since his return from the war. Time had changed his hairline but not his incomparable laugh. I loved being with him again. One day he removed the seats from his '42 Ford, put me in and drove to Pasadena, Eagle Rock, and several places on the outskirts of the city so that I could meet the members of our League of Shut-Ins living in those cities. One day we stopped at a drive-in. When ready to leave, John announced that the battery was dead, thanks to my wanting music while eating. Only Knapp would have found something in that situation to laugh about.

A drive to Capistrano almost made me a traitor to Iowa. Until we — all the Kellys and Alma — came to Laguna Beach, I had been a loyal Hawkeye. Then the Pacific, aloof yet alluring as it flirted with the shore, made me doubt my allegiance. It was a good thing we arrived at the Mission when we did.

Through its gates we passed into another world, one of strange and abundant flowers, dense foliage and winding paths. Hundreds of plump, fearless white pigeons strolled about or perched themselves cockily on a stone wall, unoccupied benches and on the heads and shoulders of the sightseers.

A brown-robed Franciscan priest showed us through a rustic chapel whose wooden walls bore the deep stamp of time. The pews, too, were worn from uninterrupted devotion. In this chapel, the "spirit of the West" was not a hackneyed phrase used to sell cowboy movies. Rather was it a tribute to gallant men — missionaries, merchants, lawyers, laborers, carpenters, cow punchers, ranchers, and railroaders — who knew the price of freedom and had been willing to pay for it.

Shortly before we left the Mission, an overweight pigeon landed on my hand, much to the delight of Andy's two grandchildren. With giggles and squeals they fed the winged visitor (who needed this meal like Marilyn Monroe needs Dale Carnegie) until I thought it would require a boost on its take-off. Finally, it lifted its wings and flew away, taking with it some of my hide. I was tempted to call a mild curse upon this scratch-and-run rascal when I saw the children were still absorbed in the bird and its destination. My wound burned like fire, but I remained silent. After all, why let youngsters of this tender age know that in this world there are many birds that can't be trusted?

Before leaving on the trip I had written Loretta Young asking if I could meet her during my visit. She had been my favorite actress for years, and in all my thoughts of being well again, I saw myself walking like Loretta Young. There was no answer until the star's secretary called me at Alma's. Miss Young would see me any afternoon at Columbia Studios!

The guard at the entrance waved us into the lot where a sentry directed us to the sound stage in which the picture "Paula" was being made. I do not know what I expected to see, but it was not what I saw. In an immense barn-like building was a set composed of three walls — one with a door. Overhead on large beams hung huge arc lights, and perched here and there on these "catwalks" were several technicians and a cameraman who apparently harbored no respect for the law of gravity.

For twenty minutes we watched Loretta Young open the door, look toward the corner of the "room" and become visibly saddened. In this scene, we were told, the star enters the nursery prepared for her baby who had died, looks toward the empty crib and wavers. She repeated this one scene about seven times, then changed into a wooly pink robe and returned to the set for the actual shooting.

Loretta Young was all I had hoped for: beautiful in every sense of the word, her eyes alert and friendly, her nose slender, her smile wide and her complexion flawless. Framing her oval face was a halo of light brown hair which was brushed into soft loose curls.

Miss Young talked to me about my work with the sick and mentioned the inspiration she had received from visits to hospital patients both here and abroad. She also spoke of her devotion to the rosary and recited the brief prayer she says each day: "Dear God, give me the courage to change the things that should be changed, the fortitude to accept those which cannot, and the wisdom to know the difference."

Through Alma's friend, Patricia Hertzog, the woman who works at R.K.O., a visit to the studio was arranged for us.

Andy called for us. Pretty Patricia Hertzog welcomed us and pointed out various departments along the street of R.K.O.'s private village. In front of an immense door, Pat stopped and asked, "Are we all here? We must enter the sound stage together or the guard at the door will make a fuss." As she checked us she discovered that Mother was missing.

A backward glance at the street solved her disappearance. Discovering that I was an arthritic, a tall extra in the costume of a Nubian slave had cornered my mother and was entrusting her with a "sure cure" — a recipe for the brewing of herbs and seeds. If we ever decided to try it, which was unlikely, one great advantage would be ours. In Iowa, a pound of alfalfa seed would be within our budget.

Shaw's "Androcles and the Lion" was in production behind the wide door. Fifty or more extras milled about in costumes that ranged from tattered beggars and charioteers to eye-filling palace habitués with Romanesque hairdos. When the director began to rehearse a scene in which a soldier throws a silver piece into a group of ragged outcasts, I watched entranced.

On another set I met and chatted with the picture's leading lady, lovely, unaffected Jean Simmons, who held her small dog "Queen Bess" in her lap. The British actor, Robert Newton, joined us briefly; then like a gale, Victor Mature blew in. This fast-talking star entertained us while a photographer was summoned. He gently touched the pink velvet headband I was wearing and smiled.

"New hat, Mary?"

"Brand new. The May Company. Just yesterday."

With a long whistle he leaned over and whispered, "Pretty darn sexy!"

The R.K.O. visit over, Pat Hertzog arranged for us to enter the Paramount lot "right around the corner." There we were taken to the sound stage where a mystery, "This Is Dynamite" was being directed by William Dieterle. I was introduced to the picture's stars — Alexis Smith, William Holden, Edmond O'Brien, and the endurable Spring Byington, who endeared herself to us by taking Mom aside like an old friend.

Our next visit was to the Metro-Goldwyn-Mayer Studios, a visit also arranged by Pat Hertzog.

We were met at the gate by a guide from the publicity department.

As Andy and John Knapp lifted me out of the car, I exclaimed in amazement: "Why it's bigger than Marcus!"

"Y-e-a-h!" John murmured, his gaze following a petite blonde. "And more interesting. . . ."

"We can go right in," the guide declared, stopping before a heavy door. "The light just went off. They're shooting 'Lovely to Look At' in here."

We were whisked inside, and once again I found myself in another barn-like enclosure.

"You can't see his face right now," our escort whispered, "but that's Red Skelton over there in the blue suit."

The guide disappeared, then returned with the famous redhead; also Kathryn Grayson, a Technicolor delight in a chic navy frock with a pink piqué collar; a trim blonde who was introduced as Marge Champion; and a peripatetic dream I immediately recognized as Howard Keel.

All the stars we had met were pleasant and gracious—with Loretta Young in a very special class all by herself. But in this M-G-M group I felt more at ease. Red Skelton was largely responsible. He rattled on incessantly, went into one of his hilarious routines, and engaged the handsome baritone in a bit of amusing horseplay.

He kept fingering an unlighted cigar, so I said, "Red, I hope you aren't letting me keep you from enjoying your cigar."

"My goodness, no!" he answered. "I don't smoke. It's too bad, too. I chased a guy a whole block for this butt."

Red Skelton needed no writers to make people laugh. The mere movement of his head, his walk, a look or a gesture, could convey bewilderment, triumph, injury, devilment, or zany deliberation, and all with a kind of comic pathos that evokes a touch of pity as well as laughter.

When our guide announced that it was time for lunch, and led us to the commissary, nothing was farther from my mind than food.

While my companions eyed the menu, I eyed the customers. From the set of "Scaramouche" yellow-wigged chorus girls glided in and out of the room in colorful colonial gowns. Mel Ferrer, one of the stars, appeared with the white curls of his pompadoured headpiece bobbing up and down on the collar of his gray business suit. Also bewigged and bewitching was Zsa Zsa Gabor, who seemed far more interested in her onion soup than in the man opposite her.

"What are you going to have, Mary?" asked the young man from publicity.

"Just chocolate ice cream," I answered in a tone which implied "and please don't bother me with trifles!"

Next on the tour was the sound stage in which Gene Kelly was both directing and starring in a production called "Singing in the Rain." Although behind schedule, he took time for a chat and an introduction to Keenan Wynn. Then with a smile and good wishes he left us.

The last I saw of him, he was in deep conference with long-legged Cyd Charisse, sultry and alluring in a costume much briefer than our visit. As they talked, apparently about the next scene, the heat from surrounding lights beat down upon them. "It must be tiresome," I thought, "but then every job has its drawbacks."

When our tour was ended, I seconded Andy's suggestion that we have dinner at Farmers' Market. But as I was pushed along the aisles of this gourmet's paradise, I wondered how I could possibly make a choice from all I saw. The vegetables and fruits were colorful, but the rows of fudge, seafoam, and panuche were almost overwhelming.

"Are you having fun, dear?" Alma asked.

"Yes, but it's a darn good thing I'm lying down!"

Andy was taking me down the last aisle when I saw it — a display of exquisitely brown roasts and fowl. My search was over. When I started to tell Andy of my decision, he murmured with mock pity, "Sorry, angel, it's Friday."

At Alma's, the feminine members of our party freshened up for the evening ahead. We were to be guests of Lawrence Welk at the Aragon ballroom in Santa Monica where he and his music makers had been breaking attendance records for more than a year.

For three hours satisfied patrons whirled around the dance floor to the music. Even Mom succumbed when the maestro raised his hand and led the orchestra in a waltz. It was fun to watch the crowd that night. Yet, as always, I felt a sort of bittersweetness which seems to be a part of so many moments that are alternately happy and sad. My mind accepts the fact that dancing is not essential to my happiness. But every now and then, especially when the rhythm is infectious, I long to glide across a dance floor as if my feet had wings.

Maybe Lawrence Welk sensed my feelings. Maybe not. But the announcement he made over the mike almost compensated.

"Ladies and gentlemen, with us tonight is a dear friend of mine from Iowa, Mary Ellen Kelly. To her, our tenor, Gene Purcell, dedicates the next number — 'Your Lovely Irish Eyes.' "

Two days later, with an orchid from Victor Mature still fresh on my blouse, I was lifted through the train window of the Los Angeles Limited. With my cot secured for the long trip ahead, I looked at my mother, took a deep breath, then suddenly blubbered like a baby. Who knew if and when I would ever see Alma, John, Andy, and his family again? They must know I was grateful. Yet I was sorry that my voice, erased temporarily by Saturday's seventeen appointments, had prevented my saying good-by to them.

Hour after hour the train streaked along — up and down mountains, over bridges, across prairies. At a time like this I missed the use of my hands more than usual. With writing and reading, crossword puzzles, and solitaire off my list, and mother, poor dear, laid low with her usual train sickness, I had little else to do but think.

Waiting for me at home would be my beloved work with the League of Shut-Ins, my writing, and the challenge it presented. Also, there were friends, Casey, my cat, and the comfortable home in which security wrapped itself about me like a cloak. The future smiled.

"And behind me," I concluded, "lies adventure."

The words struck a discordant note. I repeated them: "Behind me lies adventure." They still didn't sound right. What could be wrong?

The answer took its time coming. *An* adventure had ended, but neither it nor adventure itself was behind me: the memories of the one would be with me always, ready at a moment's notice to rout depression and loneliness. The other existed potentially in each day that lay ahead.

For adventure is finding kindness — which is a little bit of God — in human hearts everywhere. It is the unexpected, the incongruous, the spectacular.

It is a rare, personal moment of wordless communication in which race, wealth, position, and mediocrity are irrelevant. It is the animation of cardboard wishes, the awakening of sleeping dreams. It is the lifting of oneself to spiritual heights, and the pausing there to give thanks.

It is the renewal of hope, the discovery of people, beauty, laughter, and the joy of giving. It is a challenge to forgive, forget, and to be compassionate. It is a magic key that opens the soul's dark corners to an instantaneous flooding of sunlight. It is a look, a word, a gesture that conveys a mutual understanding between two people whose hearts beat in the same tempo.

It is a guard against boredom, the food of dreamers, the only outlet of realists. It is living, loving, working, sharing, laughing and, sometimes, crying. It is youth looking forward, and the aged looking backward.

It is a part of the preparation for the greatest adventure of all — eternity.

CHAPTER 15

AS I TAKE MY PEN IN HAND

For the first article I sold I was paid $5. That check was the most beautiful slip of paper in the world! I would have framed it, if I hadn't needed the five dollars. The checks that have followed have been regarded with less sentiment, but every one brings a sense of gratification — not for the money alone, but for the satisfaction of seeing my articles in print.

Until the spring of 1950, all the articles I submitted were unsolicited. Then came a letter from Father Roger Charest, a Montfort priest from Bay Shore, New York. He had read several of my articles, knew of my work with the League; and wondered if I would be interested in writing a feature to be slanted toward the sick and published regularly in the bimonthly magazine he was editing. Its title: *Queen of All Hearts.*

My YES went out with the next mail. . . .

Since the appearance of "Our Lady's Shut-Ins" in the following issue, I have never missed contributing to an edition. Though my earnings from this column are not to be overlooked, there are more important results. Having to meet the deadline does away with procrastination — a writer's biggest bugbear — and such excuses as not being "in the mood."

It is true that writing comes easier on some days than on others. Once in a great while, the words pour forth so freely that my pen cannot keep up with them. Between these "inspired" moments and those which are like digging for gold, I have no preference. Both can be exhausting; both can be rewarding.

In order to fit my article in with the aim of *Queen of All Hearts,* I studied the major work of the French saint whose teachings it promulgates. This, of course, is De Montfort's famous *Treatise of True Devotion to the Blessed Virgin Mary,* in which he presents his ideas concerning a total consecration to Mary, its nature and its effects.

The oftener I read it, the more I agreed with St. Louis that the "quickest, surest, and safest" way to Christ is through Mary. The stronger my convictions grew, the more real our Lady became to me, with my awareness of her character acutely sharpened, my confidence in her enlarged, and my love for her deepened.

A generous number of blessings followed too. I was asked to contribute a monthly column to *Action Now!*, a Sodality magazine edited by the Jesuits. This pleasant assignment I continued for three years. Next came regular features in *The Oratory* and *The Banner*, Catholic monthlies from Montreal and Chicago respectively. These two jobs still are on my schedule.

My morale was boosted by an award from the Des Moines *Register and Tribune* for "Excellent Writing" (based on my treatment of the Good Friday theme in my newspaper column "Kelly's Korner"), and another from Bob Hope—his radio nomination as "Woman of the Week." With this honor came a handsome scroll, which the Mayor of Marcus presented to me. I was also encouraged when several excerpts from "Kelly's Korner" appeared in *Cosmopolitan, Reader's Digest,* "Main Street, U.S.A.," an anthology edited by John M. Henry, state editor of the Des Moines *Register and Tribune.* And when reprints came out in the "Catholic Digest," "Stars and Stripes," and "Presidio"—an Iowa penal publication—writing became more important than ever. These were momentous events, but as my dad would say, "They don't pay for the groceries."

My love of writing would be the same if I were paid for it or not; but I can't help feeling lucky in being able to earn money from an activity I so deeply enjoy. When I learned that *Extension,* one of the leading Catholic "slicks," had accepted one of my articles, my joy was boundless. And at the sight of the check, my first in three figures, I cried. The article behind this damp reception was an autobiographical sketch called "This Side of Dawn."

To me the title bore a deep significance. It even became a sort of motto during times of pain and trouble, for it reminded me that always waiting on the other side of darkness is light — the brightness of a new day — the ultimate radiance of eternity.

The problems of writing for a living are not confined to rejection slips and heartless editors. At least for me they are not. Getting the sponge under my left wrist tied securely enough but not *too* tightly, keeping the towel supporting my right arm in the correct place, not breathing so hard that my writing board will be pushed away, and keeping my pen filled are my major concerns. As I have been writing since 1945 at a consistent average of eight hours a day, six days a week, it always amuses me when a Marcus resident, calling on me for the first time, asks incredulously, "Do you actually do your *own* writing?"

I am also amused, though not in the same way, when a well-meaning visitor carries on about how noble it is of me to spend my time writing and to earn my own way, independent as a pig on ice. Is it noble of a duck to swim? Or a bird to fly?

True, it is not with a natural ease that I fulfill this innate desire; but what of the torments women endure while dieting? Does that make them noble? No. Only slender — that is, if they keep at it long enough. And besides, if God had permitted arthritis to go on rearranging my joints, I could not hold a pen no matter how desperately I wanted to write.

As for being a breadwinner, that too is a provisional position, the provision being my mother. Without her, I could not write so much as a post card. Day after day she is on call to fill my pen, replenish my paper, hang up clippings and articles for reference, look up words in the dictionary, and adjust my writing board. This is completely aside from her usual chores of bathing me, feeding and dressing me, shampooing my hair, washing and ironing my blouses and bed linen, cooking my meals, and entertaining my guests.

While talking to my mother one day, an old friend of the family summed it up quite graphically: "You know, Bridgie, it's a damn shame you don't get mileage!"

On a blustery winter night in '55, I made an important decision

(I am getting ahead of my story but this fits in here). I determined to see if I could use an electric typewriter. When Mother heard of my idea the next day she regarded me with a puzzled look.

"But aren't they terribly expensive?"

"Yes, but I think I might get one through the Iowa State Rehabilitation Department. All I've ever asked from them is my 'Snorkel' pen."

"Well, it won't cost anything to find out."

Mother was right. Finding out did not cost anything. Before long, the machine — a demonstrator model — was delivered.

Glancing at the flimsy writing stand I was using at that time, the I.B.M. representative frowned.

"You'll need a stronger support than that for this machine," he declared. "It weighs over 70 pounds."

I had an idea. "Mom, would you please get me a heavy towel, your bread board and six thick books?"

Five minutes later the arrangement was completed.

"Okay?" the I.B.M. man asked. "Then here we go!"

When he deposited his heavy burden on the bread board, the mattress sank, my heart flipped, and Mom yelled. The typewriter had landed on her thumb.

I stared with horror at the many-eyed monster that lay purring before me.

"I know this is new to you," the stranger said in an attempt to reassure me. "All you need is a little time."

(That's what he thinks. All I need is a psychiatrist.)

"How many keys can you touch?" he asked.

I experimented, holding my breath as I stretched and strained. "With my left hand, Z, X, C, A, S, D, and F. With my right, B, N, M, the period, J, K, and L."

"That's fine!"

"But there are about 27 I can't reach at all!"

"Well perhaps as you type, your mother could move the machine back and forth."

(Or I can use only words with letters that aren't off limits.)

"With more practice you'll be fine."

The friendly young man wished me luck and said good-by.

I gave it the old school try, but it left me bruised and aching. An I.B.M. typewriter was meant for nimble fingers, not my unbending ones.

That same day I wrote another letter to the office of State Rehabilitation. Before October had run its course, I was the happy owner of a sleek, gray Dictaphone—one with only three buttons to push. Someday while I am dictating, a passerby is bound to hear me and judge that my mind has snapped.

A writer friend of mine says, "Everyone has his ups and downs. But no one has such *low* downs and such *high* ups as a writer." On a May morning in 1951 I had a phone call from Editha K. Webster, the woman's page editor of the Sioux City *Journal and Tribune* publications.

"Mary Ellen, I have some splendid news for you. . . . You have just been selected by the paper's special committee as a Woman of Achievement! Only six women are chosen a year from a tri-state area, and you have just been named as one of them. May I come over tomorrow for pictures and an interview?"

For the rest of the day, Mother and I took turns exclaiming to ourselves and each other, "I can't believe it!" We still couldn't believe it when two weeks later we attended the "Awards Luncheon" in a Sioux City hotel. I fared rather poorly at the meal (neither asparagus on toast nor creamed turkey are among my favorite foods), but little did it matter. When the guests finished eating, emcee Don Stone served me a surprise that made me forget all about food.

"And now, ladies," the young announcer began, "the moment you've been awaiting. . . . You are familiar with the accomplishments of the guests whom the *Journal and Tribune* has rightly titled Women of Achievement. From this group you have chosen the person who is to receive the extra special honor of being named Woman of the Year. Your choice . . . *Mary Ellen Kelly!*"

Mother's hand closed over mine and I think she smiled. I am not sure, because just at that time, everything blurred.

Within a month I had received more than a hundred newspaper clippings which described the occasion and pictured Mother showing me the award pin. Looking over the array, which had been taken from *Stars and Stripes*, from a Calcutta daily, the *Los Angeles Tidings*, Chicago's *New World*, the Denver *Register*, and other papers, I had a new conception of the press's power.

There also were many congratulatory cards and notes. But most likely to be remembered longest is the letter in which a friend chided:

> "I heard that you were recently named as a *Woman of Distinction*. I hope that for your endorsement, Calvert's paid you well.
>
> "P.S. In case you received any samples, make mine Scotch."

Of other awards that were to come later, the one that made me the happiest was the Christopher Award, a bronze plaque given me by Father James Keller of the Christopher movement for my article "Was I Chosen By God?" which appeared in *Woman's Home Companion* and the *Catholic Digest*. I guess it's understandable why this award meant so much to me. For with the publication of my article came a check for $1,500 and an opportunity to appear on television's Strike It Rich to pay the League's $500 printing bill. When my hand gets tired writing I think of this experience and remind my aching muscles that if they'll keep pushing, writing will pay off.

CHAPTER 16

BRIDGIE WITH THE DARK BROWN EYES

It was 11:45 P.M. when Mother wound her clock, made sure the front door was locked, turned out my bed lamp and walked slowly toward her room, only a short distance from mine. Unusually tired (I was in the midst of writing and directing a musical revue for our parish), we soon fell asleep.

But in less than an hour, a pain in my back awakened me. I tried to ignore it, but it grew worse. Mother advised me nightly to call her if I needed anything at all, so I called.

There was no answer. Again I called. . . . No answer to this attempt . . . or the third . . . or the fourth. . . . My uneasiness grew, for Mother usually wakes up if I but cough. I decided to space my calls farther apart. She had been so weary that going into a sound sleep would be natural. Or maybe she had turned toward the wall, or pulled the covers over her head. . . . Still, she had always heard me before. I called again. No answer came.

Suddenly everything changed: the shadows cast by the street light became darker and larger . . . my own breathing grew irregular . . . stillness hung over the room — and over my bed, like a cold, damp rag, and the clock in my mother's room competed with my own in noisy mocking ticks.

Afraid now to call as often as before, I alternated the calls with ten Hail Mary's. Somehow they seemed easier than original prayers, perhaps because they spared me from voicing my gnawing fears.

When another hour had passed, I could no longer conceal my terror. With all my remaining energy I cried out: "Oh, dear God, please grant that Mother is all right. Please let her wake up! PLEASE, dear God!"

Now name and substance had been given to my fears. In quiet fury they drove everything else out of my mind but one frightening possibility. Then, the very silence and darkness haunted me until I blurted out angrily: "No! She can't be dead! She just can't be!"

I cried in the silent darkness like a frightened child. New fear then moved in that bore a striking resemblance to the giant sadness waiting in me. Each one drew me into its arms and asked disturbing questions: What would your tomorrows be without her? . . . What would you do each morning without her cheery "this-is-a-brand-new-day" smile? . . . Or her special way of adjusting the pillows behind your feet? . . . Or the work she goes to on holidays? . . . Or her devotion, loyalty, and willingness to sacrifice? . . . Or evenings without her resting in her favorite chair? . . . Would Christmas ever be the same without her? . . . Or Mother's Day?

I remembered answering her impatiently during the evening and forgetting that her age and poor health warranted consideration above and beyond that owed to mothers in general. Frantic now with remorse, as well as fear, I felt my three-hour vigil reach a breaking point. At the top of my lungs I shouted: "MOTHER!"

Silence hurried into every corner of the room. Suddenly I hated this helplessness that made me as useless as a vegetable. I had never felt so trapped. Faced with a startling lack of spiritual collateral, I finally asked our Lady to accept a certain sacrifice in exchange for the favor I wanted so terribly. It was all I had to offer.

I heard the creak of Mother's bedspring. That creak was more beautiful than a symphony orchestra. Then I heard her ask with drowsy tenderness: "Do you want me, Mary Ellen?"

Do I want her! I never knew how much until that night. Agonizing as the experience was, I am grateful for it in a way, because it made me all the more qualified to tell you about my mother.

She and I are so much alike that at times our personalities clash like brassy cymbals. Each of us is stubborn, sentimental, independent, imaginative. We have a mutual sense of fun, gratitude, and seriousness. We both regard others with respect, integrity, charity, patience, and honesty. We both are partial to apple pie, old people, smoothly ironed sheets, Christmas, Democrats, aprons that are more pretty than practical, tea pots, Viennese waltzes, and Mom's golden-brown doughnuts that melt in my mouth like cotton candy. And we both dislike pepper, gushing women, liverwurst, wrestlers who gouge eyes, coconut frosting, and driving in the rain.

So far so good. But Mother, with the caution and wisdom of experience, deplores my calling my elders by their first names, buying gifts I can't afford, watching TV murder mysteries and, as she says, "writing to half the people in the United States."

She thinks I don't know the value of a dollar, yet if I wistfully mention *filet mignon*, she would spend her last cent to buy one for me. She will walk two blocks to save three cents on a pound of coffee, then scold me for buying only a yard and a half of material for a blouse.

"But a yard and a half is enough, Mom."

"Maybe so, but you never can tell what may go wrong. If you're going to scrimp, do it on something else."

This is only one of my dear mother's paradoxes. "Don't write your life away, honey," she'll advise me when I keep pushing my pen for nine hours. "You owe it to yourself to rest now." Coming from one with her inner drive, this amuses me greatly. "Work is her middle name," my dad used to say. "Bridgie Work Kelly. . . !"

Left motherless at eleven, she helped her father take over the care of his home, farm, and nine children — the youngest just three days old. Work became her pattern. When needed she helped the neighbors. Often she cooked for threshers and helped with fall canning; twice she nursed cousins who had tuberculosis.

When the Ronans moved from the eastern Iowa town of Farley to Independence, some 60 miles west, I think Bridgie Ronan's 18-year-old heart took a severe whipping. She had done everything possible to make a home for her dad, brothers, and sister, and leaving that home and the friends and places she loved so intensely was like having them torn from her. I often wonder if that experience didn't leave her with a faint suspicion of the capacity to suffer that was hers.

Grief came quickly into her married life with the deaths of her first two children. Then came a son, John Robert, a happy, husky baby whose presence set his mother squarely on top of the world.

When I came into her life five years later (also by Caesarean section), her happiness was twofold. But in a few short years arthritis stuck its ugly head into the picture. Soon it yielded space to the Depression, my brother's critical hay-fever attacks, and the death of Mom's father, sister, and three brothers. Suffering became a part of my mother in those early days. She carried her pain proudly, silently, and set for me an ideal example. Today, with diabetes, a duodenal ulcer, and an enlarged heart, she still continues to inspire me.

My lovable, stubborn mother! As far back as I can remember, our Sunday meal was as much a part of the day as attending Mass. No matter if it were 105° in the shade or 20° below zero, Mother prepared a Sabbath repast and no one could talk her out of it. Even today with only the two of us here, there is no quick snack or opening of cans. I so well remember the old routine. . . .

"Mike," our Bridgie would say just before she was ready to serve dinner, "would you like tea or coffee with your meal?"

Lifting his well-shaped nose out of the morning paper, Mike would smile behind his glasses, rock back and forth a couple of times and finally answer, "That'll be fine, Mother." Then down went the nose into the Sunday *Journal.*

One day my brother and I united forces in the hope of ending these traditional Sunday feasts.

"Gee, you look lovely this morning, Mom. Why don't you leave your good dress on and stay sort of dolled up all day?" (Not too fast. Play it cool.)

"Yes, Mother," the male member of the team joined in. "You look grand" (slowly . . .).

"How can I fry chicken in this good dress? I haven't noticed any ads for free dry cleaning."

(It's now or never.)

"Sure, Mother, let's skip the chicken today and fix up a little cold lunch!"

"You might as well save your breath, you two. Since I was eleven years old I've been fixing Sunday dinners and I have no intention of stopping now. Besides, we're not expecting company, and even if we were, I have a perfectly clean, well-starched, and completely respectable dress to put on when I take this one off, so why should I stay all dolled up?"

No filibuster ever fell flatter. Yet we were not surprised. After all, we had known her for years and should have had better sense than to underestimate our opponent.

Each time a visitor asks: "You mean that your mother lets you carry on all this League work right here — *here in your home?"* I want to shout, "Yes, thank God, she does!"

If Mother had taken a dim view in 1945 of my plan to organize the League of Shut-Ins, what empty years I would have had! Or even if after ten years she had said, "Enough's enough!" Had she done this, my life would have lost a frightening per cent of its purpose. Without League responsibilities I would have more time for freelance writing, to be sure. Perhaps all my letters might be answered promptly. But if I were separated from this work that unites hundreds of us by the common denominator of suffering, I am sure that boredom, restlessness, and self-concern soon would be my bedfellows.

If this work with the sick consisted only of writing letters of encouragement, Mother wouldn't have had to make so many sacrifices. But neither would my efforts be as effective as they are now, nor my contact with our members as warm and intimate. The reason for this is *Seconds Sanctified*, a publication that requires a daily, down-to-earth, often tiresome routine. But the performance of these very duties keeps me alert, busy, and distracted from personal aches and trials.

This same routine, I regretfully admit, robs my mother of peaceful afternoons, wears out her rugs, scuffs her furniture, uses all her paper toweling, clutters up her one big closet, and often fills her kitchen with huge boxes containing leaflets for distribution. Doesn't she ever protest? You bet she does! But ten minutes later she's likely to say, "Mary Ellen, did you write that poor old lady who wanted quilt blocks? I'll get the pieces ready, so be sure you send her a nice card!"

When people marvel at the way the League has developed, I am both proud and grateful, and silently tell our Lord so. But when someone suggests that I am doing an heroic thing, I can't help feeling guilty and even a little resentful. After all, the League is my baby (one I sincerely hope is pleasing to God) and whoever heard of a mother being congratulated for worrying about and looking after her own child? It's another story, though, where Mom is concerned. She was drafted into service.

Throughout the years it is as if I'd said, "Here's a job for you, Bridgie girl. All you have to do is provide space for an office, printing shop, circulating library, and consulting room. Just crowd these into what is now my bedroom, dressing room, bathroom, beauty salon, recreation room, and dining room. Oh — and don't forget storage space. Envelopes and paper come cheaper in large quantities."

Sometimes when Mother is exhausted from all the hubbub in the house, I wonder if the results of my work always justify the toll it takes on her. Yet, since I was a child she has drilled into me that "anything worth having is worth fighting for, and if it is worth keeping, it is worth sacrificing for." If Mother were asked at this moment if she has been taken advantage of by her afflicted daughter with the do-or-die dream, she would probably square her shoulders, repeat the above maxim, and add: "And if it is worth God's blessing, it is worth being taken advantage of by those you love."

(*Thanks, Mom, for being a grandmother to the League — my baby — and helping my crippled hands to keep it alive. Bless you too for letting me try my wings, even though I am helpless, and for taking pride in all my accomplishments. Thanks for turning your house into a testing ground for dreams and a laboratory for their development.*)

Mother has always been a tower of strength, comfort, and love. I will never forget the day I first noticed that the years were making inroads on my personal Rock of Gibraltar. I was in the hospital.

Mom was sitting by my bed, patiently listening to my teen-age troubles, when all at once she fell asleep.

"She's like a little girl," I thought, as a sense of wide loneliness crept in, "so dear and defenseless. From now on I must do all I can to save her."

And I did try to spare her. Perhaps I overdid it. Two years after my father's death I was reading aloud for her approval an article which included a passage about our beloved Mike. Unable to go on I broke down and cried.

I fought for composure and was about to apologize when Mother bent over me to wipe my eyes and said in a strange voice, "I'm glad to see that you miss Dad, Mary Ellen. I have never seen you cry since the day of his funeral and I've often wondered about it. . . ."

Her words stunned me. I thought of the nights I had waited until her bedroom light was out before I cried out my loneliness. Now I saw how wrong I had been in hiding my sorrow. Perhaps if I had shown it freely, she could have eased her own while comforting me. There are some things each of us must keep to ourselves, but since that day I have known that sadness is one feeling that must be shared.

"Your mother's a proud woman, Mary Ellen," my dad used to say. What an understatement! I admire her pride, but I wouldn't want as much as she has — partly because it has often been misunderstood — but mostly because she is never able to discuss personal problems with anyone outside the immediate family. Consequently, she has known a lot of aloneness. In contrast, I need to confide in trusted friends, just as I need friends to confide in me.

But it is that pride that keeps my mother's head high when our funds are low, her walk light when her heart is heavy, her shoes polished when the future looks dim.

I benefit from her pride in many ways. One of the most practical is our attitude toward money. If we don't have enough for something we want, we do without and no one dares gripe about it. But if that "something" later passes my mother's severe "Can We Afford It?" test, then what is purchased must be good. "You get just what you pay for," she often says.

Thanks to this attitude, I appreciate nice things but am not unhappy when I must do without. Money is an important thing, but needed only for externals. It cannot buy, for instance, the things my mother has given me.

Another benefit of Bridgie Kelly's pride is her refusal to discuss with anyone — relatives included — any difficulties or unpleasantness she faces in her care of me.

It never dawned on me that all mothers were not this considerate until a few years ago when I began to visit shut-in friends from other states. I still recall an hour I spent with a crippled blind girl and her parents. Their devotion was obvious, yet during my entire visit the mother itemized the varied services she performed for her each day. As the voice droned on, the girl sat there, quiet and apathetic, as though she were resigned to this violation of privacy.

And one time when I called on an elderly woman patient, her middle-aged daughter belabored the fact that her mother required three changes of sheets every night. As she rambled on in a martyred air, I noticed the old woman brush away a tear.

I had another conversation with the mother of a spastic daughter in her early twenties. In front of her and with no effort to speak softly, the woman told me that she seldom took her girl into public places because it was so embarrassing. "She's an eager little thing," she declared, "and loves to help me in the house. But, of course, I can't let her," the woman added quickly. "She'd have all our dishes broken."

"You must try plastic dinnerware sometime," I remarked dryly.

(*Thank you, Mom, for not carping to every caller or broadcasting my personal or physical failings, for defending me against the curious, for treating me as a member of the family — not as a crippled sparrow — and for giving me neither false praise nor false hope.*)

I can't recall when she ever placed her interests before my dad's, or my brother's, or mine. I don't advocate this practice or even approve; yet I believe that it does an invalid more good than patience, nursing skill, or an amiable disposition. The reason is simple. The fear of being a burden gnaws at every disabled person. It undermines confidence and crushes incentive. A mother who allows her handicapped child to feel burdensome by calling attention to the extra work, loss of sleep, being tied down and unappreciated, is slowly but surely squeezing the life out of him.

My mother never hesitates to show her displeasure whenever I expect too much. She minces no words when she thinks advice is due. But not once since my invalidism began has she made me feel that I am a millstone around her neck.

No example of her disregard of self means more to me than the prompt and cheerful way she answers my middle-of-the-night summons.

"Is there something I can get you, honey?"

"Sorry to disturb you, Mom — especially when you're so tired — "

"Tired?" echoes this nightgowned angel of mercy. "Who said I was tired? I never felt better!"

After an aching knee has been rubbed, an aspirin administered, or a pillow adjusted, she asks if I'm sure there's nothing else. Then with my bed light revealing the lines etched by worry, work, laughter, disturbed nights, and tears, she smothers a yawn and reminds me that "it's no trouble at all" for her to come in again if pain "or anything else" bothers me. The light disappears and noiselessly (she never takes time to put on her slippers) she returns to her empty room.

(*Thank you, Mother, for not making me feel that I am more than you bargained for. Thank you for your insistence on clean linens and for declaring that washing clothes is no trouble, for scolding me when I need it, and for allowing me to make the big decisions by myself. Thanks again, Mom, and bless you!*)

CHAPTER 17

SAME SONG, NINTH VERSE

THIS was my ninth trip to surgery. I looked around at the familiar operating room and the unfamiliar eyes of the masked crew who staffed it, and felt strangely calm. Not that I was brave; I had simply run out of fear — just as one runs out of tears.

Before Mother and I left for California, my doctor had advised me that surgery was necessary to avoid certain internal complications. As always, I accepted his decision without question, and postponed thinking about it — a helpful trick learned as a younger patient — throughout our trip and the Christmas holidays. Then, abruptly, an overpowering fear took hold of me.

Oddly enough, it was neither the pain nor my usual post-surgery nausea that frightened me. It was fear that the operation — the dislocation of my left hip socket and the insertion of a steel plate — would jeopardize the relative comfort into which my joints had been "frozen." Over and over a warning hammered into my brain: *Let well enough alone!*

Even though further tests confirmed the doctor's diagnosis, I was still unconvinced. Out of my very queasy apprehension I asked him a question: "Doctor, if I were your own daughter, would you still recommend surgery?"

I saw the hurt surprise in his face and felt sick. "Dear God," I prayed, "I didn't mean to hurt him! Let him know I didn't mean to hurt him!"

"The operation is entirely up to you," he said in cold reproach. "Think it over and let me know what you decide."

I was nagged by remorse for doubting him. For five days I hit a new low in misery. Finally, in a kind of weary capitulation to the inevitable, I decided to take the trip upstairs. An hour later, Betty Van Cleave, a lovely graduate who had offered to special me, rushed in with a message. "The doctor's nurse phoned, Mary Ellen, and asked me to reassure you that everything will be fine — not a rough deal at all. She said to tell you that it would be just like falling out of bed and breaking your hip."

In the week that followed the operation, I seemed to be in the midst of a losing battle, with doctors, sand bags, nurses, oxygen tanks, transfusion equipment, needles, bandages, and emesis basins on one side, and I on the other.

The struggle pulled me one way and then another. Fatigue seeped into every muscle until all I wanted in the world was to surrender. But each time I reached this point of no return, Mother's voice penetrated the haze around me. I could not see her, but I heard her say again and again, "This is Mother, darling. . . . I'm right beside you. . . . *Please* fight a little harder, Mary Ellen, won't you try for Mother. . . ?"

The tide of battle finally changed but the feeling of emptiness and inertia persisted. One morning after my blood pressure had nose-dived, the big man stormed into the room, sent the window shades rolling upward, and growled, "What's going on in here? Put that radio away! She's got to fight!"

For the first time in four days I felt a sensation other than exhaustion. With the force of my entire Irish ancestry behind it, I *boiled.* I waited until the man in white left the room. Then I exploded.

"Fight, my foot!"

I learned later that my doctor had been gruff purposely to rouse me. He succeeded.

While waiting for strength to return, a new fear moved in. Why had I been so reluctant to fight? Did it reveal a kind of cowardice — or worse — an existing fraud? If I were as happy an invalid as I had believed myself to be, then why was I so tempted to close my eyes and escape forever from that weird pain and hollowness?

As soon as I felt better, I knew I had been foolish in attaching a moral significance to my post-surgery attitude. Once in the comfortable lap of convalescence, I wanted to live for a hundred years.

On Washington's birthday another doctor performed minor surgery on me in my room. My discomfort was dimmed by a heart-warming surprise — a dollar shower! When the crisp, green bills fell out of the first five envelopes, I credited it to a happy coincidence; but as the pile grew, so did my astonishment.

"You have a lot of friends, dear," Mother said.

I agreed, but a lump got in the way of my saying so.

The days wore on, some of them lonely, some crowded with visits from former hospital friends. There were new friends, too, with Betty Van Cleave heading the list. And there were high school girls who helped me answer a portion of my League of Shut-Ins mail, a pretty red-haired night nurse, a Negro girl who had mischief in her eyes and springs in her feet, and a Polish orderly who had miraculously escaped from a Siberian labor camp. Their good wishes, problems, and company shortened the long days.

It was difficult to adjust myself to idleness. Being flat on my back, with my feet elevated, made writing impossible. But there was one thing I could not adjust to — something that would last forever: the way my left leg was moved out to the left. It was the first thing I saw when I came out of the anesthetic, and the sight of it — at least twenty inches away from the other leg — brought a rush of tears.

"Don't cry, darling," Mom comforted.

"But, it's so — so *unladylike!*"

Eventually, I ran out of tears, but I still felt sad and embarrassed every time I looked at it. My new position caused more than intangible problems, as we were soon to learn. When I was lifted onto the cot for the first time since the operation, my leg stuck out six inches over the side.

"Holy mackerel!" I moaned. "How can I ever again squeeze through a train window?"

March 22: Same song, eleventh verse . . .

"Do I get a prize, Doctor?"

"A prize?"

"Sure — like those that are given to the millionth customer in a store or restaurant. This is my eleventh trip up here to surgery."

"Oh, I see. Okay. You get a nice fast anesthetic!"

"Humph!" I snorted. "Who ever started that rumor about the luck of the Irish?"

This operation, in which my collarbone was removed, took longer and was more complicated than anticipated. The bone had become swollen and was pressing against nerves and muscles. But its removal brought such relief that asking any questions about it never occurred to me. A friend asked me, "Kelly, how can a person live without his collarbone?"

"Gee, I never thought about it," I replied, "but Doctor will know."

When he heard the question he laughed. "Your collarbone? Don't give it a thought. It's only something to hang your coat on!"

Now that all my surgical remodeling was completed, I wanted to leave the hospital. I missed home and all that it meant to me: solace, privacy, an elastic routine, popcorn on Friday evenings, the smell of fresh apple pie, communication which does not depend on words, a precious feeling of united conspiracy, protection, second helpings, encouragement for budding dreams, comfort for broken ones. Home was a cathedral in which love nestled in every corner and faith sustained all those who dwelt therein.

When told that Perassos' ambulance was waiting, I begged God's forgiveness for my inadequate appreciation, asked Him to bless those who had cared for and cheered me, and the Sisters of Mercy and County officials who had assumed the expense. Then I thanked Him heartily for giving me a home and a mother to return to. Even for my pet cat, Casey.

During those thirteen weeks in the hospital, I thought a great deal about resignation. I have also thought about it since and, as a committee of one, feel obliged to defend that misunderstood and maligned word.

It is not a stupor or a rest period, as many seem to think. It is not a cessation of activity, an unconditional surrender in the face of overwhelming odds, or a gear with which one pushes himself into indifference, there to coast along for an indefinite length of time.

Resignation is a pin-point peak which can only be reached after prodigious climbing. A person cannot relax his caution, even when he has reached the top, for so lofty is the height and so delicate the balance that an instant of carelessness can plunge the climber earthward. Fortunately, the oftener he tries to reach the heights, the greater his courage becomes. But as each attempt means passing along a new route, complete with its own obstacles, the climb never becomes a cinch, a joyride, a mere pastime for a dull day. There's no chance to show off with, "Look, Ma, no hands!"

A popular misconception is that in such outlets as anger, love, jubilation, and vindication, intense action is sustained. This is not true. At most, it is prolonged only for a short while, its very nature being explosive. No outburst of anger lingers on and on; it either expends itself in quick violence or fizzles to a slow-burning resentment.

Though love itself is a movement of the intellect and will, it frequently lends itself to similarly active but brief manifestations. As regards jubilation, a moment of intense joy can be replaced in an instant by pain, sound, memory, or the sudden realization of what the moment has cost.

Resignation is different. If the activity it requires were set to music, only in the perpetual motion theme of *Hora Staccato* might one find an adequate interpretation. Meeting this prerequisite is no easy matter, even though one believes that it brings necessary happiness both here and in the hereafter, and has long tried to practice it. Take me, for instance. For years I have known the facts about being resigned; but in order to stay that way I frequently have to put myself through this third degree:

1. To what must I resign myself?
2. What does it involve?
3. What will be gained from it?

Unless I am so deceived that I can only rationalize, the answers are quickly reaffirmed:

1. I must resign myself (with our Lady's help) to God's will.
2. It involves a simple admission that He knows more than I do; it means suppression of my own desires in deference to God's, and the constant effort to turn these desires into channels which lead

to my salvation and to the spread of God's honor and glory.

3. God's pleasure and blessing, peace of mind, possible inspiration for someone in dire need of it, the satisfaction of utilizing my life, performing the important job of reparation and, if I stick to it, of winning heaven, which is no bad exchange.

Anyone who thinks that resignation doesn't require intense and sustained activity is also likely to believe that resignation is easy. Take it from an old mountain climber who has incurred multiple bruises — it is just a little easier than teaching a toadstool how to rhumba.

By the same token, one who believes that resignation is not worth all the energy, sacrifice, and self-annihilation which it demands, has never known the incredible and sweet benediction of Him who resigned Himself not only to the ignominy of a stable and a cross, but also to the contempt of those who would again order His execution.

I have never heard this elusive virtue extolled more eloquently than by Monsignor William Boyd. It was on the occasion of his elevation to the rank of a *Domestic Prelate* that this crippled priest, since 1950 the spiritual director of our League of Shut-Ins, wrote me these words:

"I was completely overwhelmed by the announcement; never in my wildest dreams did I expect to receive such an honor. Though years now weigh on my shoulders, and my pulpit is only the microphone used in my Sunday broadcasts, gladness floods my heart — unworthy vessel that it is. Yes, you may tell the news to our white-robed martyrs in the League — those precious, uncomplaining victims of love. Let them be cheered by this reminder that God does not forget these hidden souls whom He has chosen for Himself. Let them take renewed hope from these purple robes, seeing in them a promise of the mantle in which Christ will enfold them on that glorious day when there will be no more tears, pain, or loneliness. Then, held tightly against His bosom, their limbs now straightened, eyes sighted, ears attuned to sound, and maimed bodies made whole, they will commence an eternal thanksgiving for having said: 'Not mine, dear Lord, but Thy will be done!' "

CHAPTER 18

A ONE-WAY STREET

I HAVE tried to push the subject of resignation aside in order to continue my story, but ever since I completed the preceding chapter, a dozen questions have been begging for an answer. Now I find that of all the virtues, submission is not only the least easy to understand, it is also the most difficult to explain.

Too often I have become irritated at my failure to convince someone that I do not consider my illness the greatest tragedy of the century. The last time I tried to do this, my listener regarded me sadly and said: "My dear, you are really wonderful. This act you put on — this pretense to be happy — is simply remarkable! But my dear," she purred in an intimate *we-have-a-secret* tone, "you can't fool me: I know how you *really* feel!"

Before I could answer, she asked, "How long have you been crippled?"

"Since 1939."

"And you're resigned to it, aren't you?"

"Well," I replied, "after all these years, I'd be pretty stupid if I weren't."

Apparently missing the inference, she gave a couple of "tsk-tsks" and added, "It's a shame — a *real* shame — that you've given up!"

I wanted to set her straight, but I was no longer naïve enough to believe that I could make anyone with such distorted reasoning understand.

Then and there I resolved to let skeptics think as they wish. I can't force my beliefs upon anyone; I desire only to describe, as honestly as I can, my attitude toward my invalidism and the happiness I have known in spite of and because of it.

First, then, the question of giving up. To restore me to health, my parents did everything they could, sparing themselves nothing. So did several doctors — especially the orthopedic surgeon who first diagnosed my illness. When it became evident that their combined efforts had failed and that no more could be done for me, I soon realized that I would be an utter fool not to make the most out of the energies and pleasures left for me to work with and enjoy.

God has helped me become resigned to these limitations. By no means, however, does this willingness to accept my condition imply that I *want* it or that I am against doing all I can to become well. It simply means that I believe my handicap to be in God's plan for me, and that until such time as He may decide otherwise, it is my duty (as well as to my advantage) to try to co-operate with His plan and to do so without complaining. If this is to "give up," then I am guilty.

Another common misconception is that physical discomfort is the only thing an invalid has to overcome. Is this a laugh! Generally speaking, pain is neither the only nor the hardest thing to overcome. While no part of the distress and unpleasantness caused by my physical dependence is easy to take, some aspects require more courage and adjustment than others. And some hurt more, too, like knowing that the privilege of motherhood will never be mine. Yet even this hurt is not of constant duration — my life is too full and busy to allow that. Neither have I ever been (I am thankful to add) jealous of women blessed with children. In fact, sometimes the worry or grief in a mother's face makes me realize that motherhood often brings as many tears as it does smiles. (Still, it seems to be a gamble that most women are willing to take; I know I would be.) It might seem like negative thinking that I should derive even a fleeting sense of relief for having been spared that kind of sorrow. But while lying on my back I have learned never to refuse a legitimate consolation, even a brief, opaque, or left-handed one.

Unfortunately, all the resignation in the world doesn't prevent a dull, potential emptiness from creeping into my heart. It's a strange feeling — somewhat as though I were looking down the long corridor of time to find a child that might have been. Searching carefully behind each tomorrow, I try to glimpse that face or hear a footstep, knowing all the while that no one is there — that it is a search without hope. Like a sleeping cat this expected loneliness crouches somewhere within me, quiet and motionless, but ready at just the right provocation to spring into attack and, in the same moment, send a plaintive cry throughout my being.

Sometimes I am able to ignore this recurrent theme; other times it is an echo that haunts me relentlessly. But regardless of what I feel, I firmly believe that the sacrifice I have been asked to make is not too high a price to pay for admittance into the paradise that awaits far beyond time, far beyond the last tomorrow.

Once when I was disturbed by doubts, I received guidance from a La Salette priest friend. Our conversation, which I remember as though it took place yesterday, went almost exactly like this:

"You know, Father, the idea of never having a child is one I can live with. Sure, it hurts at times — plenty — but like all hurts, it eventually passes. So, this I can manage, as long as I keep the facts straight and don't get tangled up by rationalizing. But what bothers me — what I can't figure out — is this: is it wrong for me to feel this way in the first place?"

"Absolutely not!" the priest declared. "Such reactions are completely normal. So are your regrets at being unable to bear children. If you felt otherwise, you would be less of a woman."

"That's a relief!" I admitted with a sigh. "But that's only half the problem. . . ."

"I'm listening. . . ."

Putting the other half of my problem into words was no easy task. After several attempts I finally blurted out, "How in the world can I want two exact opposites at the same time — and each so badly?"

Father looked puzzled. "Two opposites?"

"Yes, that's right. To do what God wants — be an invalid — and to be what I want — a wife and mother. Did you ever hear of anything so contradictory?"

"Isn't human nature full of contradictions? As Bishop Sheen once remarked when giving the definition of a cross: 'The vertical bar is

God's will. The horizontal bar contradicting it is our will. When our will is in conflict with God's will, we have a cross.'

"In other words, to want such things as love, marriage, and family is part of our nature, placed there by God; therefore, these things can't possibly be wrong. Only if your desires lead you to rebel against the Divine Playwright would an offense be involved. You may not always like the part He has written for you — and for you *only* — but if you accept it, that's what counts! And if you try hard, you might even find yourself conforming to His script, keeping your suggestions for a rewrite to yourself. Stranger things have happened."

"Well, I think I'm trying, Father, but sometimes I can't help feeling that if I loved God as much as I should, this other sense of unfulfillment would disappear — or at least decrease. Don't you think so?"

"You forget something," he answered. "If this feeling weren't present, or if it caused no pain, then where would be the sacrifice?"

"No cross, no crown, you mean?"

"Exactly! Think of it this way. In my opinion, God has very special plans for you. We all have one obligation in common . . . to know, love, and serve God. We accomplish this by reproducing in ourselves, as best we can, the most perfect image of Himself. This in turn is done by developing and utilizing all the gifts and powers of soul and body, plus the material things which He has placed at our disposal, in the most perfect conformity with His law and under the inspiration of grace.

"In all His wise Providence," he continued, "God sets two main paths along which all are called to follow. It is along these paths — which are the ways of celibacy and marriage — that He wants us to walk through life and, in walking, to climb ever nearer to Him until the day when at last we pass through the doors of eternity and enter into the glory of heaven.

"Then, Mary Ellen, He who was seen while on earth, as St. Paul says, 'dimly as in a glass,' will be seen face to face in 'all the revealing light of eternal radiance,' and there will be perfected the union begun on earth through sanctifying grace."

"You express it beautifully, Father, and what a picture of hope you draw! But what did you mean about there being two paths?"

"They aren't hard to understand. The person called to God through the marriage state travels the path we call 'the holy, spiritual, and beautifully graduated steps of human love.' The person called to celibacy," he went on, "is required to approach Him in a more direct manner, sacrificing on the altar of love for God, not only all illegitimate pleasures, but *legitimate* pleasures as well, in favor of a *more perfect and more direct surrender to God*."

"Golly," I replied thoughtfully. "I never dreamed that all this lies behind the vows of every priest and nun!"

"Not only priests and nuns, Mary. Don't overlook the people in the more recently formed Secular Institutes and those who, though not possessing a vocation for either of these, forego marriage in order to dedicate themselves to doing God's work."

"Yes, Father, I see what you mean. And then there are others like me — neither fish nor fowl — "

"That's what you think! The category you're in is the most exclusive of all!"

"What?" I asked incredulously.

The priest laughed, then answered patiently, "Men and women like you — those whose circumstances of life exclude them from marriage — have an advantage the others have not: they are absolutely sure of God's will in this regard."

"You mean no other celibate can make that statement?"

"For them," he continued, ignoring my interpolation, "there can be no doubts or uncertainties as to whether they have correctly understood God's design for them. *They are sure!* As surely as God chooses His priests and nuns, He has chosen *you*, Mary Ellen, to throw yourself directly into His arms through the practice of perfect chastity!"

I had to think over his words, slowly fitting them to my needs. As though he understood my silence, the perceptive missionary said, "Don't expect to embrace these truths all at once, Mary. Give yourself time — give *God* time! Make your heart receptive to His love and let Him win you how and when He desires. Remember, too, that He is a jealous lover and will not give you up easily. In short, don't select from His wishes only those that suit your taste. Instead, you must accept *His* terms and forget about making conditions. In your case, He asks for complete surrender."

For a moment I regarded my friend without speaking. "Father," I said at length, "you could have made a million as an attorney for the defense!"

He grinned. "Isn't that what I'm trying to do — plead God's case? I've heard on good authority that the pay for this job is very rewarding, and the best part of it is that its amount is based not on whether one wins or loses the case, but strictly on the effort put forth. A good deal, wouldn't you say?"

"The best," I agreed, "and if it's any satisfaction to you, you've convinced me. If only I could enforce my convictions, I'd be sitting pretty!"

Suddenly, as though my wish had signaled them, disturbing memories marched before my mind's eyes and ears . . . a radiant bride standing on tiptoe to straighten the tie worn by her adoring groom . . . a friend's laughing remark that I was the only girl she knew with whom she'd trust her husband . . . that fifth-wheel feeling that changes a gala evening with married friends into an uneasy one . . . the embarrassment of a pretty girl who abruptly interrupted the detailed account of her engagement with a remorseful "Oh, I'm sorry! I hope I haven't made you feel bad!" . . . lonely vigils on New Year's Eve . . . the curiosity of an unwelcome visitor who asked if I ever got frustrated and, if so, what I did about it . . . a pig-tailed two-year-old, curled up on the bed beside me . . .

Then, as suddenly as it had started, the parade of memories stopped. Something was beginning to dawn on me. These moments to which my invalidism had given existence had seemed empty, painful. But as I had long ago offered God my *heartaches* as well as physical ones, I suddenly knew they had not been futile or wasted. I also realized that these heartaches would be replaced with new ones, and that this cycle would be repeated as long as I lived. Therefore, the sensible thing to do was to accept them as they came and offer them to our Lord through His Mother. If I didn't nurse or dramatize them, they would pass and be forgotten.

Father coughed. "Are you still with me?"

"Forgive me! I was thinking about the case you've put before this one-woman jury."

"I see. And have you reached a verdict?"

"I have. I am guilty on three counts: not loving God enough, not trusting in Him enough, and not praying enough to disprove the first two charges. I hope the Divine Judge will be merciful; this isn't my first offense, you know."

The priest stood up and blessed me. "You can always count on our Lady to enter a plea of clemency," he said reassuringly.

"I'll remember that, Father."

I have remembered it, too; in fact, my La Salette friend would be rather surprised if he knew how often his words help when my reasoning blurs and my will power buckles. For he has made me see that being single is *not* the worst thing in the world, even though it is not of my choice. A lot of women are in the same boat — and not all of them are invalids, either.

So also has this priest's advice and explanation led me to realize that God is an eternal Lover who is never unfaithful, selfish, or unjust. He loves me in spite of my weaknesses and fears; He forgives my failures when I am sorry. He knows my needs better than I do and generously offers graces to overcome them.

I have failed Him often, and probably will again. But with His help, perhaps I can learn to face with courage and patience the obstacles that clutter this one-way path which God has laid out as my particular route to heaven. And when I get lost, the guideposts erected one day by a La Salette missionary will help me to find my way back.

CHAPTER 19

IT PAYS TO ADVERTISE!

TEN days before Christmas, 1952, Betty Van Cleave and I boarded a train for Chicago on a very special mission. I never think of it without laughing, for although that wintry trip had much to be happy about, it started off on a dour note.

I arrived late at the Sioux City station and saw Betty and the Perassos waiting for me. Quickly Tony and Bill signaled their embalmer, Kenny Adams, and together they whisked me out of the station wagon. They de-wheeled my cot and hoisted me onto a baggage cart. Seconds later I was being aimed at a train window that couldn't possibly admit me unless my left leg was to remain behind.

"Try tipping her!" someone shouted.

My heart keeled over. "Golly, NO!" I protested. But my countermand was competing with a shrill train whistle.

"Sorry, kid," Tony shouted. "It's the baggage car or nothing. . . ."

I looked at Betty. "How about it gal? Are you game?"

"S-s-s-ure!" she shivered, her nose almost as red as her lipstick.

The relieved and slightly irritated conductor signaled to the engineer, and we were off. I blew the snowflakes from the end of my nose and sighed. This was a far cry from the observation car in which I usually traveled. Why, of all days, did it have to be absent?

The gallant man in charge of our drab quarters gave his low slung canvas-backed chair to Betty and told us to let him know when we wanted dining-car service. Glancing down at the box lunch at the foot of my cot, I smiled at our host and murmured my thanks.

When he left for a few minutes I whispered to Betty, "If he thinks we're going to fork over $3.50 apiece for a meal when we can feast on Mom's fried chicken, he's looney!"

From the depths of her fur coat, Betty answered something that sounded like "You said it!" Then, leaning toward me to reach the box of food, she gave a startled scream as the back of the chair fell forward and conked her on the head. I couldn't help laughing.

She brushed off her angora beret and buried it and her matching mittens deep under my blanket. Easing back cautiously into the chair which she no longer trusted, she sighed. Later, she pushed two trunks together and went to sleep on them. But my mind was too preoccupied with our trip to Chicago to sleep.

P. W. O'Grady, executive director of the Confraternity of Pilgrims, was determined to conduct a pilgrimage of invalids to the two most renowned shrines in the world — Lourdes and Fatima. He had met with opposition and discouragement from just about everyone he contacted, but finally he put it over. He was ready now to announce publicly that the trip was scheduled for September, 1953, nine months hence.

I came into the picture because I had shared Mr. O'Grady's eagerness to provide American shut-ins with this travel opportunity. Besides, I had long wanted to go to Lourdes, and the thought of Fatima held a more recent but even greater appeal. So when that determined Irishman outlined his plan to me, I pledged my services for whatever they might be worth, and told him he could count on one reservation for sure.

A lot of eyebrows were lifted when this news circulated around Marcus. Everyone in town knew that I could barely afford a round trip to Sioux City. To this day I don't know whether my announcement stemmed from implicit faith, childish optimism, or plain old colossal nerve. But Mr. O'Grady must not have had any doubts about me, for he asked me to lead the pilgrimage (as I had done in 1946 on the first invalids' trip to Canada) and help publicize the tour.

The Confraternity staff arranged for me to appear on "Welcome Travelers," a coast to coast radio program over C.B.S. It was emceed by Tommy Bartlett and broadcast from the College Inn of the Sherman Hotel, Chicago, where reservations had been made for Betty and me. I wasn't afraid of being on the show, yet so much depended on my appearance that each turn of the wheels made me wider awake.

At Chicago's Union Station, my dear fire fighters retrieved me from the baggage car and pushed me into the immense waiting room. Before I could introduce Betty to the Confraternity group, I was introduced to Peter Wright, a handsome young *Herald-American* reporter who fired questions about the European trip, the purpose of the Chicago visit, and my attitude toward suffering. At that moment I was sweltering under a second wool blanket placed on me solicitously by Fireman Stanley Zellak, and I wanted to say that it wasn't the pain I minded as much as the humidity. After several pictures were taken in front of the station's towering Christmas tree, we said good night to the members of the fourth estate and headed for the fabulous Loop.

Come to think of it, that almost perfectly describes what my heart was doing that happy winter night.

Early Monday morning, December 15, I reported to the "Welcome Travelers" headquarters where I was greeted by the affable producer, Les Lear, and briefed on the show's format by a sour-faced script writer. Tommy Bartlett, a stocky, young man with a Boy Scout grin, appeared next on the scene. After one more rehearsal, all I had to do was wait.

At last I was cued on stage, and before I could get too scared, Tommy was telling me the gifts that his sponsors wanted me to have!

"For your trip to Europe we have a three-piece set of Samsonite luggage. Also a Parker pen and pencil and a year's supply of stationery with your name engraved in gold."

I was groping for words of thanks when I heard Tommy mention my mother. ". . . and for her — she's pretty important to you, isn't she? — we have a dozen pairs of nylons, three lace-trimmed slips, and three dresses in the latest fashion . . . and according to our reports, I believe this is something your mother will love . . . a new double-tub Dexter washing machine!"

"Oh, that's wonderful, Tommy!" I interrupted. "Mom hasn't had a new machine since I was a little girl!"

Again my thanks were interrupted. "For your lovely companion," Tommy went on, "we also have a gift — a genuine leather, fitted handbag by Evans and, as a special surprise for you — a five-unit intercommunication set for your home. . . ."

It was hours later before I came down to earth. In all my life I seldom won anything, not even at bingo. Now a veritable avalanche of gifts had been heaped on me. Tears and laughs were all mixed up inside me. My sentences sounded like dialogue from "Alice in Wonderland." But by lunch time when my party and I were the guests of "Welcome Travelers" in the luxurious Porterhouse Room, I was able to select my meal with extreme care.

At dinner that evening one of the waitresses whispered to me, "Did you notice that girl in the wheelchair when you came in?"

"Yes I did. Isn't she pretty?"

"I'll say. She would like to know if you're a paraplegic."

"Well, no I'm not. I have arthritis. Is she alone?"

The waitress nodded.

"Would you ask her to join us? There's no need for her to be alone."

The lovely dark-haired girl deftly maneuvered her chair next to my cot and introduced herself. The moment she spoke, one could almost smell honeysuckle, for she had the southernest southern accent I had ever heard. After several tries she finally made us understand her name — June Bryant (it sounded like Brown). She was twenty-two, paralyzed from the waist down as the result of an auto accident five years earlier, and had just returned from Rochester, where she had undergone surgery for about the twentieth time. She was taking a plane for Alabama the next afternoon.

Quietly, almost shyly, she accepted my invitation to return to our room with my friends and me, and joined the parade across the lobby to the elevators. There was scarcely a word out of her; then the ice broke when a cousin wanted to treat us all to highballs and asked Betty to phone the order to Room Service.

Betty was doing fine with the various names of drinks until she asked June what she would like.

"A Mahscow Meyoull," the southern belle replied.

"A *what?*"

"Mahscow Meyoull," June drawled carefully.

The third time it dawned on me. A Moscow Mule! I translated it for Betty and added, "Make it two. This calls for a toast to the Confederacy!"

Almost unbelievably, she emerged from her timidity and became the life of the party. When all the other guests but one left, things simmered down a bit as conversation headed into an inevitable subject — our respective handicaps. Each of us approached it guardedly. Finally June asked if I had ever worn braces.

"Did I! And were they a nuisance!"

"Did ya'll have walking lessons too?"

"Oh brother!" I groaned. "They scared me so much the nurses heard me holler way up on the fourth floor!"

"Did you take them fo' quite a spell?"

"Five months (it seemed like five years). It was useless to continue though, because the only way I could go was backward, and everyone knew that that was dangerous."

"Ah should say so! You could easily fall that way."

"No, that wasn't the reason. If I kept walking backward, I never could have faced reality."

An awkward silence followed. Why on earth, I thought, did I pull such a corny gag? I was groping for a remark to cover up, when June's lips parted in a smile that worked itself up to a delightful laugh. That did it. From then on there was no more hedging.

Describing the rehabilitation school she had attended, June told the misadventures when she was learning to do household work from her wheelchair, drive a car, get into one unaided, and pull the chair in after her. As she recounted these hilarious escapades, her eyes sparkled as brightly as the gold gypsy-like earrings that tossed back and forth against her fluffy hair. Her wit, timing, and sense of the ludicrous would have entertained us until dawn if Ann Pedersen, our other guest, a friend from Marcus, had not laughed until she fell off her chair at 3 A.M.

"I surrender!" she cried, tears rolling down her cheeks. "One more story and I'll never make it to work!"

She disappeared under the bedcovers, and Betty saw June to her room. While waiting for Betty I thought of this crippled girl who a few hours earlier, had wheeled into my life and into my heart. Did she have moments of longing to flee that confining chair? Did anger nibble at her when she absent-mindedly conveyed to her feet a message they could not obey? In view of her gaiety and take-each-day-as-it-comes philosophy, it would not seem so, and yet invalids are often masters in the art of masquerading. As a matter of fact, some of them put on a performance so frequently they are unable to distinguish the real from the make-believe. It was strange that I was unsure which way it was with June. But then once in a while I am not even sure how it is with me.

We met June for lunch the next day and learned that she had been asked to stay over and appear on the "Welcome Travelers" radio program the following morning. Her mother had already been notified of the delay and another plane reservation made. June acquitted herself ably the next day, and among her gifts was an intercommunication set, which seemed to her a heaven-directed choice.

"Now when ah fall out of mah cheah in the closet, ah can jus' *send* my mothah the message!"

Four hours later the gifts were forgotten as Betty and I said good-by to June and watched a cab driver help her into his cab. I hadn't known her long, nor was it likely that I would ever see her again, but the impression made on me by that southern charmer would neither be erased by time nor dimmed by memory.

The possibility of my being on the new "Welcome Travelers" television program had been mentioned (this show originated from a Chicago theater transformed into a TV studio), but as no further word had come, Betty and I concluded that our stay in the city was over. We spent our last cent on a shopping spree that left me with a deepened understanding of the thirst of gold. With packages piled on me so high that I couldn't see my feet, Betty and Clara Gerner,

Mr. O'Grady's executive secretary, took their place at either end of my cot and pushed me up Randolph Street. At each corner a heavy-coated policeman hurried to help lift the cot off the curb. We suspected that they were motivated less by chivalry than by fear of what we might do to the 6 P.M. traffic.

Mr. O'Grady was waiting for me at the hotel. "Good news!" he exclaimed. "You have another chance to publicize our pilgrimage to Europe!"

"I do?"

"Yes — Austin Kiplinger is going to interview you on his *Daily News* television program, *Impact*. How soon can you be ready?"

The damp air had taken the curl from my hair and the starch out of my blouse, but Betty could offset the damage if anyone could. With an orchid to top things off, I was ready for anything — and soon.

A knock at the hotel door concluded my primping. Seeing Firemen Dan Cahill and Timothy Patrick Twohill in the doorway, I said happily: " 'Tis honored I am to be escorted by two such elegant spalpeens! Maureen O'Hara never had it so good!"

Mrs. O'Grady joined us a moment later, and the safari to the lobby began. When the smiling doorman peeked through the ambulance window and called "Have a good time," I smiled my thanks and added silently, "Mister, I am!"

Friday was a day for miracles. Awakened by the phone, Betty lifted the receiver reluctantly, said "Hullo" and yawned. Then she sat bolt upright and, with eyes popping, carried on a weird conversation comprised mainly of yesses.

"Mary, guess what!" She replaced the receiver and whirled around. "That was the secretary from 'Welcome Travelers' and you're invited to be on their *television* show *this* afternoon! She'll check back with us in ten minutes."

I stared at Betty in disbelief. Being on network radio was one thing, but on coast-to-coast *television?* Me?

"Aren't you thrilled, Mary?" asked Betty, puzzled by my silence.

I tried to answer but I was speechless — and in more ways than one. The damp air had sabotaged my voice. "Betty!" I whispered in horror. "Of course, I want to be on the show, but how can I when I can't talk?"

Betty went into action. Unfortunately, her efforts failed: so did the anti-cold tablets I prescribed. With a superficial confidence, I maintained that all would be well, and then stormed heaven not to nullify this miracle.

As soon as the camera crew agreed on the position of my cot, Tommy Bartlett and Announcer Bob Cunningham sat beside me for a brief run-through. Hoping to sound casual I whispered to them, "I have a little cold."

They must have thought that I was trying to be secretive, for they replied, "Then you better not tax yourself. Besides, you're an old hand at this."

But thanks to the good Lord, no subterfuge was necessary. Though my voice wouldn't have soothed an infant to sleep, it at least conveyed my message. Then, believe it or not, when the show ended, so did my voice. The gifts that day were a beautiful wrist watch for Betty, and for me two handsome occasional chairs and a *television* set! If I had not already been speechless, I would have been.

Remembering this eventful day, I often wonder where the energy came to enjoy as I did the anti-climax which Frank Bering, manager of the Sherman, attached to it. For that evening at the Great Northern Theater, no three could have laughed louder at the Phil Silvers revue, "Top Banana," than Betty Van Cleave, Fireman Norman Young, and Mary Ellen Kelly.

PART 3

CHAPTER 20

OPERATION DREAMBOAT

THE TIME:	Sundown, September 27, 1953.
THE PLACE:	Pier No. 5, Hoboken, N. Y.
THE GIRL:	Me (too scared to swallow).

THE time had come. This was the moment I had waited for and dreamed about. "I can't believe it," I told myself. The truth is I didn't want to. And *I was scared green!*

How was I ever to get aboard that giant whale of a ship lying in the dusk? Was the water always so black? And how will they get me off the ship — that is, if they ever get me on?

Nine months earlier I had told my friends, "It's definite. Next September the Confraternity of Pilgrims will conduct the first nation-wide Pilgrimage of Invalids to Europe, and I, God willing, shall be among them."

"You?" they repeated.

"Or a reasonable facsimile of same."

That New Year's resolution was foolhardy, to say the least. I was solvent enough to obtain my passport, but how could I pay for my passage? My beloved Betty Van Cleave could obtain a leave of absence to go as my nurse-companion, but the trip would put her in debt up to her eyebrows.

Many persons warned me of sea sickness, the hazards of inexperience, an outbreak of war, shipwreck, a stolen passport, and/or physical collapse.

"Are you sure you want to make the trip?" Mom asked. "Real sure?"

"I've never been surer of anything."

"Then you had better get busy. No one is going to hand you the money and say 'Bon Voyage.'"

But they did! Kind friends in Sioux City and Marcus gave two "Silver Teas" for me. As a result, one thousand 'Europe-or-bust' dollars were put into my hands. The rest of the money came too — sometimes from most unexpected sources . . . and joyfully, thankfully I sent for my reservation!

Between writing deadlines I daydreamed; between duties as nominal leader of the pilgrimage, I designed new blouses; between visitors and calendar watching, the reluctant months made way for September, New York, and Pier 5. . . .

Five days ago our train slid into Grand Central Station with the grace of a Willie Mays stealing home. In our compartment I looked up into the faces of Mother, Betty, and my dear friend from early hospital days, Mary Jackman Burns, who had come all the way from Denver to see me off.

"This is it!" I said.

My companions were silent, but the look in their eyes showed that they understood my excitement, and hoped that nothing would break the happy spell I was under.

New York! The city glamorized by Park Avenue, victimized by racketeers, itemized by Dun and Bradstreet, fictionalized by Damon Runyan, motorized by hurried drivers, eulogized by George M. Cohan, immortalized by the Yankees, and bought from the Indians for $24.

Before leaving Hotel Commodore for Long Island, where we were to spend our five pre-sailing days, Mother, Mary, Betty, and I had the pleasure of meeting one of the greats of show business — Joe E. Brown. Later we joined the *Queen of All Hearts* editors, the Montfort Fathers. They arranged for us to stay nights with a neighboring family and days at the Montfort Consecration Center in Bay Shore, the birthplace and home of the magazine which features my column. Quickly, carefully, the Fathers and two laymen from the Center de-wheeled my cot and hoisted me into their station wagon as the Commodore doorman looked on. I expected to be taken directly to Long Island, but I was in for a surprise.

From my window-viewpoint dozens of places I had seen only in the movies or in my imagination suddenly appeared in glorious reality: Central Park . . . a shining hansom cab . . . Broadway . . . Times Square . . . 42nd Street . . . Carnegie Hall . . . Madison Square Garden . . . Wall Street . . . the waterfront . . . Chinatown . . . the Bowery . . .

"And this," one of my hosts announced, "is the Fulton Fish Market."

As if he had to tell me.

Next came Coney Island — a broad expanse of littered ground bounded by water, cluttered with pop stands, saturated with the smell of pizza and — on this late September day — haunted by the dreams of countless summer patrons who came seeking escape either from heat or reality.

Jones Beach, even more deserted, wore the sad, lonely look of an abandoned playground. Its gigantic parking lot, naked without its usual thousands of cars, lay quiet in the semidarkness, like a concrete desert.

The remaining fall days whizzed by like Manhattan traffic. There were many callers, an "open house" held in honor of the Iowa guests, more sight-seeing, and peaceful hours spent near the canal on the Montfort property. There was also a visit with the League's Charter Member of Newark, Betty O'Brien, a devout and talented spastic, and with the priest author, Father Francis Beauchesne Thornton.

And reporters! Again and again I had to spell "rheumatoid." Yet I was glad, for publicity helped to dispel the idea that invalids are prisoners. Also it would spread the message of "Operation Dreamboat." When I gave that name to the project, I didn't dream it would stick as it did. Thanks to A.P., U.P., and the NCWW, the name traveled even farther than I.

Now we were on the pier. I looked from the ship to the water and back again. My New York stay had been thrilling. Maybe no one would think it *too strange* if I — well — eeled out of the overseas trip. . . .

There wasn't time. I was whisked to another part of the pier where I saw my invalid co-travelers for the first time, with photographers and newsmen swarming about them. Uniformed nurses, police, and firemen threaded in and out of the increasing crowd while a group of the curious gathered around each cot and wheelchair. I could glimpse the top of Betty's hat, but Mother and Mary were lost in the crowd.

"Here she is!" The deep voice belonged to the Confraternity's executive director, Mr. O'Grady, who had fathered the entire invalid travel movement.

"Am I glad to see you!" I declared. "What a crowd!"

"Mary Ellen, I'd like you to meet Father John Weisbrod, a port chaplain here in Hoboken. We have him to thank for this tremendous reception and send-off."

"How do you do, Father — "

My words were lost as two broad-shouldered policemen made a quick getaway with my cot. Moments later they deposited me into a roped-off section of the pier which I recognized as the site for the Mass soon to be offered — the first evening Mass in the history of the Newark archdiocese. Other invalids were wheeled up to form a front row of wheel chairs and stretchers.

Bishop William Nelligan of Canada celebrated the Holy Sacrifice before an estimated two thousand persons. Afterward, His Excellency Thomas Boland, Archbishop of Newark, gave a brief talk to the afflicted.

A musical program kept the crowd entertained while relatives gave last minute instructions to us soon-to-be voyagers. Mother must have had a hundred warnings to impart, but couldn't speak a word. And all I could think of was: "How will I be put aboard (a derrick, maybe?)"

Don Ameche, bless his heart, at this moment pushed my transfer problem into the background. By letter he had accepted my request to come to Hoboken to meet the Confraternity members. Now here he was — handsome and debonair — with his attractive wife, Honore. We chatted like old friends until a loud announcement interrupted: "Members of the Pilgrimage of Invalids are to board the Nieuw Amsterdam *at once.*"

Mother gasped. Don Ameche quietly said, "We'll follow you." The volunteer entertainers stood on the improvised stage with their eyebrows up and their instruments down. Betty ransacked her handbag and demanded desperately, "Where *did* I put our passports?"

The policemen with my cot were heading for the gangplank.

I closed my eyes . . . and prayed.

I opened them when my cot again rested on something solid. In five seconds I had been transported to an enchanted kingdom. I wasn't sure how it had happened, but as I stared openly at the gleaming hallways and luxurious furnishings, I was awfully glad I'd come.

A tall, uniformed purser interrupted my appraisal.

"Dis way," he directed graciously.

(Probably a duke in disguise, I mused.)

The two policemen and I followed him to the elevator and went inside, only to find that the length of my cot prevented the doors from closing.

"Den we go down da stairs," the accented voice said evenly.

As strong hands carried me down thickly carpeted stairs, young princes masquerading as stewards passed beside me and smiled broadly. At the foot of the stairway the stately purser waved us to the 2nd class cabin assigned to Betty and me.

"Oh, oh!" one of the policemen warned again. "With that extension at the foot of her cot, it's too wide to get her through the door."

"Come. Follow me," the accent commanded once more. "We try an odder cabin."

More stairs. More princes.

"Here we are. Dis should do it."

(It should have, but it didn't.)

"You'll have to do better than this," I heard Don Ameche say, as the officers squeezed me into a narrow passage between two beds.

"Yes, sir!" the accent agreed. "I am sure something more accessible can be arranged."

Still more stairs. On one of the decks we passed my faithful Montfort friends. "Hi!" I called as I joggled by.

"Hi!" they chorused. "If you ever land, be sure to write!"

I was about to ask what was par for the course when the next try met with success. I had landed in a first class cabin! The policemen lost no time in mopping their foreheads, wishing me a safe trip, and departing. (I hope their backs weren't permanently impaired.) Mother admired the spacious accommodations I had innocently acquired, but remained unconvinced of the ship's ability to stay afloat. Reluctantly she said good night, assuring me she'd be back the following morning to see Betty and me before our noon sailing. The Ameches and my loyal band of "old" friends bowed out next, leaving Betty and me alone.

"Will morning ever come?" I asked her wistfully.

"Too soon! Too soon!" she cried, and collapsed on the bed.

I realized that being unable to get into the elevator would change the plans I had made for the following morning. For me there would be no fading-from-port scene, no waving of handkerchiefs, no salute from the Statue of Liberty. But compared to what would come later, I wasn't too disturbed or disappointed. I couldn't wave at anyone, anyway.

CHAPTER 21

THE ATLANTIC, THE DUTCH, AND ME

"THE Atlantic, the Dutch, and me!" With this combination, contentedness snuggled into every square inch of me. Strains of afternoon concert music floated up from the lounge, and from the ocean — stretched out before me until it ran into the sky — came a symphony of sea sounds that could easily have lulled me to sleep.

But of sleep I wanted only a minimum. I told Betty, "We'll have eight days on the bounding main, and I don't want to miss a thing!"

From morning till night one could be occupied, if one so desired. And I did. Our day began with Communion, then a siesta on deck, lunch and a group conference conducted by the pilgrimage director, the genial Father Richard A. Cahill, S.J., pastor of Milwaukee's Gesu church. Then a concert, dinner, the rosary, a movie, and an informal chatter session in one of the sumptuous lounges.

We also watched the dancing, live turtle races, and the horse (cardboard!) handicaps. Santa Anita spectators could scarcely have shown more excitement. Largely responsible for my happiness aboard ship was the wonderful Dutch staff. When Mr. O'Grady wrote that all (Europe-bound) ship lines but the Holland-American Line had refused to accommodate so many disabled passengers, I naturally became prejudiced in favor of the *Nieuw Amsterdam*, the Holland-American's flagship.

Now I had come to love the proud liner carrying us to the old world. To me she embodied the strength, character, and pride of the Dutch people who built and sailed her. Like her staff, she knew war and suffering, but was not clinging to them or wearing their souvenirs in public. Like the men who guided her, she knew the secrets of the tides and the treachery that often voids centuries of ocean mastery.

Because of her immensity I never felt in the way. Even in the theater my cot didn't block the aisle. I felt that I was a passenger first, an invalid second. Among the ship's crew I found friends I shall always remember and love: Arie Breestraat, a 19-year-old Netherlander, tall, handsome, capable. He was the ship's carpenter, and obligingly enlarged my cot's footboard which saved my toes a thousand bumps. We found much to talk about in spite of language difficulties — especially after he said he didn't believe in God. He spoke about his mother, brother, the war years, his hobbies, the qualities a man ought and ought not to have. Day by day our friendship grew, and everytime I looked at Arie's strong yet sensitive hands, I wished it were possible for me to bring him to America for the right training to develop the talent being wasted on a routine job.

In regard to Arie's denial of God, he contradicted his statement before the crossing ended. Confident it had been prompted only by hurt and confusion, rather than any deep-rooted conviction, I was more pleased than surprised when, just before disembarking, he hurried over to me and quietly said, "When you come back to ship, I hope you have a miracle and will be walking."

From one who doesn't acknowledge God, a miracle is wanted?

Arie is now married to a lovely girl. He has put the sea behind him and is working hard for his wife and son. He may never make Rotterdam's *Who's Who*, but I'll wager that the Breestraats will rate high in "Who's Happy."

Rita Geldof, our stewardess, was an attractive young woman with dark blue eyes, a wide friendly smile and short curly hair. She told of sacrifices and hardships with simple matter-of-factness and no self-pity.

Each day I learned something new and surprising about her. I'd thought of her as getting what fun she could out of living, with little care above the future or obligations. Then I learned she had been in love a long time but had postponed marriage in order to contribute to her mother's support. I loved to have Rita feed me because each session gave me another piece to fit into my picture of her. Sometimes with her I wished I had held tighter reins on my heart. Once it takes a real fancy to a person, that loved one can run away with my affections, and it had taken more than a fancy to Rita. She was wonderful to me, yet at times I wondered if to her I was simply another passenger. One evening in my cabin I found the answer to my doubts.

We had been talking about all the things we can do without and still be happy — in my case, health and movement. Just when I expected Rita to answer she suddenly turned her head so that she was no longer in my direct line of vision. Finally she turned and faced me.

"If I hear one day that you can walk," she said tensely, her eyes filled with tears, "that will be the happiest day of my life."

Across from a snapshot of Rita taken aboard ship, my scrapbook has a page handsomely decorated with her wedding picture, taken in 1954, and the announcement of her son's birth in 1956. Each time I see these mementos I am reminded that I wasn't just another passenger.

Kees Vreeswyk was a sensitive clown in a steward's uniform. At war's end, this slight fellow, with the kind eyes and Chaplin-like stance, retained his sanity through the one treasured thing the Nazis could not destroy — his love of music. I could picture Kees on a podium, directing a symphony orchestra. Or in a conservatory teaching musical interpretation to eager young minds. But I could see him as steward and elevator boy only when he stood before me in that capacity.

When not playing the buffoon — a role he portrayed skillfully and to the delight of our pilgrimage group — Kees performed his duties with a friendly tolerance, and then returned to the world he loved — music. He allowed a few persons a glimpse into his private world, but it was obvious that he lived there only with his wife and his music.

Thanks to Kees, the problem of the too-short elevator was finally mastered. By leaving the inner gate open and operating the switch with his knife, he could take me up and down with the greatest of ease.

Hank Wind was a suave deck steward with a coldly realistic attitude and a warm heart that often must have complicated things for him. One evening we were discussing people, whom I maintained were fundamentally alike and shared the same basic fears, hopes, emotions, when Hank gave me a cold look and declared stonily: "You are hopelessly naïve!"

"But Hank," I insisted, "if I were blind from birth, what possible difference could I detect between men of different colors? And if I were deaf, how could a different accent or language influence my judgment? Aside from these externals, people are — well, *people* — each person a miraculous combination of body and soul."

Hank toyed with his cocktail for a moment before he answered. "I don't know if I could ever come to think like you, Mary, but I believe you are the most cosmopolitan woman I have ever met."

That's better than being naïve, I thought.

Hank's latest Christmas card announced the opening of his own hotel. Remembering how he smuggled my luncheon tray on deck so I could prolong my sunning, I feel confident that he is doing exactly what he wants to do: making people happy.

I had known only one of the pilgrimage group personally — Dixie MacMaster — the Canadian Charter Member of our League of Shut-Ins. We had once shared a pilgrimage to the Canadian Shrines, and now were elated at being shipmates. Irene Krokos was a pretty polio patient from Chicago who had been an iron lung captive for months. She radiated the joy of liberation from her mischievous eyes down to the only toe she could wiggle. Dorothy Zettle, the other cot case, was more reserved. However, she didn't miss a trick. Until this trip Dorothy, a victim of muscular dystrophy for 30 of her 32 years, had never ventured beyond her home town of West Branch, Michigan. Now she was embarking on a journey of ten thousand miles!

The wheel-chair travelers were Jean Macauley, a Toronto graduate of McGill University and an undergraduate of multiple sclerosis; Lucille Ramstack, an Elm Grove, Wisconsin, patient with the same disease; two charming Dominicans, Sister Joseph Claire and Sister Kathleen Dolores, and Janet Muth of Yonkers, New York.

At sixteen, a diving accident destroyed Janet's control of arms, hands, and legs. But her fine mind and visionary spirit were in no way impaired. In Yonkers she spearheaded drives to give Christmas baskets to the needy and held story hours for children twice a week at the City's Women's Institute. She even raised funds to redecorate the Institute's reading room, which now bears her name.

Six months after our pilgrimage, Janet Muth was to return to France to enter the Congregation of Jesus Crucified, one of the few religious communities admitting invalids exclusively. The congregation had great plans for its talented and zealous Sister Marie Ombeline. But so did God. At sixteen she was asked by Him to surrender her physical independence; at 30, her will to His; at 33, her life.

Also in our group were twenty or more ambulatory members—some with heavy crosses. We couldn't have done without them, nor would we have wanted to. And yet our special unit on wheels remained curiously apart from the others. To us, each day revealed miracles of surprise, satisfaction, and reprieve which only the physically fettered could appreciate. For instance, the ship's gentle swaying rhythm held a very special thrill: by closing one's eyes, one could easily pretend to be dancing—even those of us who couldn't walk.

When we were ready to dock, Betty exclaimed: "Imagine—in a few moments we'll be landing at Le Havre!"

"I wish I didn't have to get off the ship."

"Mary Ellen! The pilgrimage is just beginning!"

But so was something ending. No more around-the-clock holidaying. No more hours watching the mysterious Atlantic. No more Rita, Kees, Arie, or Hank, who might or might not be on the return crossing.

Feeling a leaden lump of pain at the thought of not seeing them again, I placed them in the hands of Our Lady, Star of the Sea. When my enchanted kingdom floated away from Le Havre, leaving me behind on the dock, the pain was still there.

CHAPTER 22

FROM PARIS TO PARADISE

"PARIS," I had told myself, "will greet me with flowers in her hair and a cluster of acorns on her copper-colored gown!"

Instead she wore the black dress of darkness, shook soot in my face and rolled out endless railroad tracks rather than a red carpet. Actually, it wasn't her fault. At Le Havre we invalids took one look at the narrow train windows and resigned ourselves to the baggage car for the three-hour ride to Paris. . . . Too jostled to sleep and too keyed up to daydream, we were saved from complete boredom by Janet Muth, who looked out of the tiny window above her wheel chair and gave us a running commentary on passing scenes. Just before night spoiled our fun, she peered through the dusty glass and declared, "French cows are just like American cows!"

And at first, Paris seemed just like any other city. I was pushed through a dark station by a puffing French volunteer who groaned as he helped lift me into an outdated ambulance. It started with a tired hiccup, lumbered noisily through the streets, and stopped with a jerk in front of a rambling hospital, our quarters for the next four days.

Inside, I glanced about the long ward shared with Dorothy, Janet, Betty, a French patient, and six empty beds. "Hmph!" I snorted. "We came to Paris to see the Seine, and what do we see? A hospital! For this we crossed the Atlantic?"

"Well, tomorrow's another day," sighed Betty.

On that philosophic note I decided to go to sleep. "Maybe I'll dream about some handsome French poet," I thought as I mentally turned on my side and drew my knees toward my chin.

The next day our group toured the city in buses ideally suited to invalids. We gawked, gasped, cooed, craned our necks and spent our money whenever we could delegate some robust soul to dash into a shop for a quick purchase.

What is Paris like? She's an ageless woman who is many things to many people. To the patronizing she's a faded *ingenue;* to the naïve, a sloe-eyed Jezebel. To those wanting to flirt she's the chaperone who winks and turns her back. To those wanting only to forget, she offers a thousand distractions.

She's a hostess who welcomes her guests graciously, then runs them down by screeching taxis. She houses her art treasures in the marble halls, while her meat and poultry hang openly in the blistering sun. Sometimes regal, sometimes a coquette, she wears the past with dignity and the present with one eyebrow arched. She's imprudent, crafty and outspoken, but never, never dull.

Each time I returned to the hospital I thanked God I was not a permanent patient there. Breakfast in the ward was a bowl of tea and a chunk of bread whacked off a long loaf held tightly under a nurses's arm. Being neither a tea nor bread fancier, I was indebted to Kees for the can of peanuts he'd given me before we disembarked. Each morning I slowly ate a few of those golden nuggets, washing them down with a bottle of warm Coke. A stack of pillows at the foot of each bed took the place of blankets, which were all right providing one didn't have sore toes. There were no call lights for signaling the nurse, no washbasins, no service trays, no napkins. But standing proudly under each patient's bed was a bottle of wine. Maybe two.

"These people do without a lot, Betts," I said one day. "But then after three or four swigs of wine, who cares?"

Away from the hospital, Paris continued to enchant me. On her streets old women hawked flowers and picked up cigarette butts. People with time on their hands rested their feet at sidewalk cafés, while those in a hurry dashed for streetcars already spilling over with arms and legs. At 4 P.M. the Sorbonne emptied itself of bearded youths and pony-tailed girls. At 8, the city put on her most brilliant jewels and dazzling gown. Then with a cloak of darkness draped casually around her, she stepped forth onto a rich carpet of chestnut leaves, and, like a queen, smiled at me as she extended her hand in greeting.

At *Rue de Bac* we saw the lovely Apparition Chapel in which the Blessed Mother appeared in 1830 to a young nun, now St. Catherine Labouré, and asked her to propagate devotion to the Miraculous Medal. Her incorrupt body lies beneath the side altar. Encased in glass, her mortal remains are startlingly visible to all who wish to see as well as to those who do not wish to understand.

Exposed in a large reliquary near the other side altar is the heart of St. Vincent de Paul, one of God's noblest servants. I looked at that preserved heart, once ablaze with love for Christ, and prayed that the feeble flicker in mine would grow one day into a steady, glowing flame.

The Paris tour at an end, Betty packed our belongings. Picking up a box of souvenirs, she thumbed through the top layer and asked with a nostalgic catch, "Hasn't it been terrific, Mary?"

"Golly, yes! I still can't believe I've seen the Louvre, Champs-Elysees, the Eiffel Tower. . . ."

"And the Palais Royal, Sacré Coeur, and Notre Dame. . . ."

"And the Arc de Triomphe, Maxim's, Montmartre. . . ."

"That's right," Betty interrupted: "You really went for Montmartre in a big way! Was it because of the chestnut trees?"

"Chestnut trees, my foot! Montmartre's the only place in the whole darn city where I found a cold bottle of Coke!"

Paris wore a drowsy look the morning we left. As we headed for the station in the dim light of dawn, my thoughts weren't on the city I'd probably never see again, but on a friend named Robert Lax — poet, journalist, and roving editor of the excellent publication *Jubilee*. I had met him on our third day in Paris, a meeting that climaxed a four-year correspondence but was unfortunately cut short by hospital rules. I took this annoyance in stride, also the disappointment of missing still another visit. But when I missed out a third time it proved too much for my spirits to ignore. Even Betty was infected by my *mood indigo*, for she shared my opinion of Bob.

I first read about Robert Lax in Thomas Merton's *The Seven Storey Mountain*. To Merton, Lax was "a kind of combination of Hamlet and Elias. A potential prophet, but without rage. A king, but a Jew, too. A mind full of tremendous and subtle intuitions, and every day he found less and less to say about them, and resigned himself to being inarticulate. In his hesitations . . . he would often curl his long legs around the chair, in seven different ways, while trying to find a word with which to begin . . . and the secret of his constant solidity I think has always been a kind of natural, instinctive spirituality, a kind of inborn direction to the living God."

My one meeting with Lax confirmed everything Merton had said about him; also the opinions I had formed from his letters. I knew that I had been privileged in meeting him personally, yet I couldn't help regretting that I had been absent the night before when Bob returned to the hospital. Now in the midst of these thoughts I heard Betty shout, "Mary, look! It's Bob Lax!"

There by the train stood this thin, bareheaded Marian troubadour. "You're a hard one to find!" he said with a warm smile.

My depression melted away, and as soon as I was safely aboard and lowered between the two seats of our compartment, Bob joined us. The thirty minutes we spent with him fully compensated for my earlier disappointment, although I wished this last meeting didn't have to end quite so soon.

"I'd better see if it's about time to get off — "

Before he could untangle his long legs and step out of our cramped quarters, the train slid out of the station without so much as a lurch, a whistle, or a roar. Aware that the first stop on our long journey to Portugal was all of two hours away, I tried to conceal my gladness as Bob, slightly bothered and bewildered, stuck his head back into our compartment.

"Be my guest," I invited.

He didn't have much choice.

His return to Paris must have been without mishap, for in a few weeks, from the French Capitol, I received a bank draft from Bob Lax for exactly twice the amount of money I insisted he take with him to return to Paris.

We arrived at the Portuguese village of Albergaria in late afternoon. Thirty-four hours of being wedged between two train seats had exhausted me, and a severe cold rattled in my chest like a sack of marbles. I was weary of idle hours and scenery and of "compartment hoppers" who dropped in to chat just when I had fallen asleep.

Gray skies. Rain. Flat Spanish plains with occasional clumps of greenery that clung to the barren earth as though stubbornly exercising their squatter's rights. More rain. More flat plains.

In no mood to brave an open-eyed transfer from the train to the ambulance waiting to take me to Fatima (about 20 miles away), I closed my eyes as usual going out of the window and left them closed until safely inside the small station house. When I opened them, my old fear and new miseries were soon forgotten.

Poverty nodded her head everywhere I looked. Crowded on benches and standing on every available space were old women and young women clutching black shawls tightly about them. Some had no shoes on, but all wore gold earrings. Only their stooped backs distinguished the aged from the young.

I realized that I was staring at them. I looked away, but I could feel them staring at me. Looking back once again, I found myself warmed by what I realized was compassion, not mere curiosity.

The ambulance window framed the desolate scenes that led to our destination: tiny one-room houses with earthen floors, outside stoves and thatched roofs . . . red clay-like soil stretched out for acres in a peaceful siesta . . . here and there a sapling with its pockets slashed . . .

Yet all this evidence of poverty did not depress me or fill me with pity. The next day, October 12, explained why.

From the Retreat-house balcony overlooking the entrance to the shrine grounds, Janet Muth and I braved the chilling midday wind to watch a drama unfold. Below us on the main road, one bus after another discharged passengers who, like us, had come to honor the Mother of God and seek from her a special favor. Others arrived on bicycles, burros, and donkey carts, while still others came on foot with a bundle of belongings balanced on their heads. Some of the native Portuguese were barefoot and some had a child strapped to their backs. There were busloads of pilgrims from Austria, Germany, Belgium, France, Italy, England, and Australia. There were women from India, priests from Africa and the Orient, and individual pilgrim travelers from at least ten other countries.

This human stream, ever widening, ever moving, made its way past our balcony and on toward the vast piazza that faces the Basilica and adjoining hospital. We knew from our morning tour that many of these devout souls would then climb the Basilica steps on their knees, often leaving behind a fine tracing of blood.

Inside the Basilica they would kneel at the side altars before the entombed bodies of Jacinta and Francisco Marto, two of the three children to whom our Lady appeared six times in 1917. As Mary predicted, the brother and sister died in their youth. Lucia, their cousin who also witnessed the miracles, is today a cloistered nun.

Then, like Janet and me, these hopeful pilgrims would be drawn like a magnet to the statue of Our Lady of Fatima. There at her feet they would try to give expression to the love, contrition, and gratitude within them; then lay before her the innermost longings of their hearts. . . .

This much of the drama Janet and I had experienced as we viewed the scene below. Until the second act took place late in the evening, I wanted only to absorb the atmosphere of these hallowed grounds and learn from our *Servita* the high lights of the events that have startled the world.

It was in 1915 that the story began. Three peasant children were playing when the oldest, Lucia Abobora, noticed a strange white something that moved majestically from east to west, far over the valley, and then disappeared. Lucia was teased about this "vision," so she preferred not to speak of it.

On May 13, 1917, Lucia's young cousins — Francisco, then nine, and Jacinta, seven — were permitted to accompany her on her duties as shepherdess. Coming to their favorite place, the Cova da Iria, a kind of natural bowl amid the hilly district near Fatima, they saw a ball of light and in the center stood a Lady. As Lucia describes her she was "all of white, more brilliant than the sun dispensing light." Finally she spoke to them: "Don't be afraid, I won't hurt you!"

Lucia then asked, "Where does your Excellency come from?"

"I am from heaven," was the melodious reply. She told them to come for six months in succession on the thirteenth day at that same hour. Before leaving them the Lady said, "Say the Rosary every day to obtain peace for the world and the end of the war."

In Rome, on that same day, Msgr. Eugenio Pacelli (the late Pope Pius XII) was consecrated Bishop at the Sistine Chapel.

As she promised, the Lady appeared again on June 13 and July 13. By now, the news of the visions had swept Portugal. Ti Marto, father of Francisco and Jacinta, guided his children wisely during these months, neither exploiting nor punishing them. In August he suffered a severe blow when his child and Lucia were temporarily jailed with thieves, rapists, and drunks.

For the October apparition a crowd of seventy thousand gathered. Because the people could not see the vision as the three children beheld it, they grew angry. Suddenly the sun cast weird colors down upon them and became seemingly detached from its orbit. Afraid that it was falling on them in a dizzy spin, the crowd screamed, fell to their knees and begged God's forgiveness as a torrential rain spilled upon them.

When Lucia tried to escape from the mob, a young man from the village carried her on his shoulders to a safe place. That same man was to carry my cot out of the Basilica exactly thirty-six years later.

In less than two years Francisco was dead. Jacinta died in 1920. Lucia entered the cloistered convent where, as Sister Marie of the Sorrows, she revealed her identity to no one except the superior until it was made known to her that her role was not ended.

On May 13, 1928, the cornerstone of the Basilica was laid in the very spot where the children had first seen the Blessed Mother. Entombed in the two front side altars are the remains of Jacinta and Francisco Marto. When their bodies were exhumed in 1935, Jacinta's was incorrupt. Her cause for beatification has been introduced.

When our *Servita* went inside I knew why the poverty had so puzzled me and why I felt such greatness in this place. By modern standards these people have nothing, but measured in terms of faith, they are wealthy. Long on sacrifice and suffering, they are short on malice, duplicity, and greed. I realized now why I was so impressed with our ward in the Retreat-house. It had no heat or warm water; one naked light bulb hung from the ceiling, and its mattresses and pillows were straw filled. Yet the moment we entered I sensed its humble beauty.

I wondered what thoughts were uppermost in the minds of my wardmates. Jean Macauley and Lucille Ramstack . . . were they dreaming of a miracle that would strengthen their legs and steady their arms? . . . And Janet — what desires were locked behind her humor and good disposition? . . . And Angeline Wood, an older woman from Texas — was she hoping to return to her ranch minus the cane that supported her . . . ? And my dear Betty . . . She had no problems health-wise, but what human heart has everything it wants? Was she thinking about the nice young court reporter I had introduced her to in Chicago? Could he be the one whose shirts she wanted to iron the rest of her life?

And what of me? Did I want a miracle? As the wind blew against my face, I viewed the conflicting beliefs and desires that had followed me to Fatima. I had to find an answer soon.

To a well person it must seem strange that I could have any doubts about wanting to be cured. But I did, and at times the struggle had me on a mental teeter-totter. Explaining why won't be easy, but I shall try.

I had been bedfast four or five years when it became clear to me that I react to things in one of two ways: as *Mary Ellen-woman,* and as *Mary Ellen-invalid.* Having my hair set evokes the first reaction; being fed evokes the second one — especially when soup spills down my chin. Toward a beautiful sunset, my reaction is a combined one, my normal appreciation increased by the confining periods in which I see no sunsets at all.

In time I realized the necessity of distinguishing these reactions from one another and of interchanging them. A remark to make

Mary Ellen-woman laugh might make *Mary Ellen-invalid* cry, so even though I would be experiencing the latter reaction *inside*, I would be making every effort to regard it outwardly as nonoffending. The more accustomed I became to this practice of analyzing my reactions, the more distinct they themselves became. And when the question of a cure arose, I soon developed into a battleground.

As *Mary Ellen-woman*, I regarded a cure as most anyone would expect me to, thinking with pleasure about clothes, dancing, dating, marriage, and a family. Strange as it may seem, it was the pilgrimage that brought these thoughts into sharp focus. Otherwise they appeared only occasionally — though intensely.

To *Mary Ellen-invalid*, a cure meant the end of having to ask for my every need, of countless annoyances and sacrifices. It meant being able to comb my hair, relax in a hot bath, brush my teeth, sleep on my side, make a private phone call, open and hold a personal letter all by myself, kneel when I prayed, attend Mass regularly, blow my own nose, and a thousand other things I would dearly love to do. A cure meant a respite for Mother from all the extra work I caused her, to say nothing of the anxiety and heartaches.

Since a cure decidedly appealed to me both as an invalid and as a woman, these two reactions caused no conflict. During the early stages of my illness the thought of God and His will became a conscious influence on my daily life. For years I tried to regain my health. I even asked for and consented to painful surgery considered beyond the "ordinary means" we as Catholics are morally obliged to take to preserve our health and life.

Then came a point when medical science admitted that no more could be done. I was a permanent cripple. Having been trained from childhood to accept God's will, I interpreted my invalidism as the expression of His will for me. And as I had also been trained to add an "if it's God's will" to all favors, I tacked it on to all my prayers for a cure.

There was nothing extraordinary or sanctimonious in this. God must know what was best for me. A cure might lead me into more trouble than I had bargained for. Besides, as I was convinced that no one enters heaven without a cross, I wondered if I were being wise in asking God to exchange the one I had and was used to for one that could very well be much worse.

Mary Ellen-invalid had still further qualms. In eight years the League of Shut-Ins had become so interwoven into my life that the thought of giving it up left me depressed and lonely. Once a cure was granted me, *I wouldn't even qualify for membership in my own organization.* This thought haunted me. I had been able to help them *because of my own helplessness,* and in asking for a cure I was deliberately withdrawing this help. It seemed selfish.

Such were my thoughts on the balcony at Fatima. Annoyed at my indecision, I was about to give up when a solution appeared. *I would ask for a partial cure!*

This was a perfect answer. If I could use my hands, bend my elbows, sit up straight and turn my head, I would be more comfortable, less dependent on others, and able to do a great deal more. Yet I would still be an invalid, still doing the work I was pretty sure God had cut out for me. This indeed was the answer, and in view of all He *could* do, I didn't think He would hesitate to grant such a reasonable plea. But that, of course, was up to Him.

By late afternoon the piazza was teeming with people. A young layman from Glascow elbowed a path through the crowd as two other Scots, both scholastics at the Fatima seminary, pushed me toward the small chapel housing the famed Pilgrim Virgin statue. "One of the apparitions took place here," Fausto Ferarri told me, though I could have guessed it from the expressions of the prayerful pilgrims who were coming this way on their knees across the huge courtyard.

"They really love the Blessed Mother," Danny Thompson observed. "In fact, they think of her as *their* Lady!"

"Yes, I've noticed that already," I said, "and in spite of the deep happiness and peace I have here, I feel somewhat like an intruder."

Vincent Goldstein, the bearded scholastic, regarded me with the suggestion of a frown on his intelligent face. "Mary wouldn't want you to," he said soberly.

Simple words, but they had a strange impact coming from one who had been a Jew.

Darkness and rain descended on the piazza together. Onto a hundred thousand people they descended, each person carrying a lighted candle and singing the hymns whose words appeared on the paper globe that shielded the flame.

Betty and I joined in the procession, but my cot kept bumping into a native pilgrim kneeling in prayer or huddled beside a sleeping child. I wanted to take an active part in this pre-feast day observance, but from the sidelines it still was a magnificent spectacle, and for me a safer one. So I watched under the protection of the Retreat-house and trembled at the sight: children . . . soldiers . . . mothers-to-be . . . the blind . . . the lame . . . nuns . . . priests . . . bobby soxers . . . aged women . . . bearded men. They encircled the piazza slowly, singing, praying, while flickering candles flashed a story of love and reparation.

"Some of this throng will crowd into the corridors of the hospital and the vestibule of the Basilica," our volunteer helper or *Servita* explained, "but most of them will sleep tonight in the rain."

"But won't they catch cold?" I asked anxiously.

The *Servita* looked at me in surprise. "With our Lady looking after them? My goodness, no! When it doesn't rain, they think she is displeased with them, so they are glad for this chance to sacrifice. In fact, when the piazza was laid with concrete in 1950, the native pilgrims were heartbroken: they felt that the mud under their feet offered a better opportunity for penance than clean, solid cement. How our Lady must love these humble servants!"

The darkness finally left, but the rain stayed. From the window in our ward the piazza resembled a wide sea, with a multitude of umbrellas creating the illusion of floating mushrooms. I didn't mind rain as a rule, but against this downpour I had developed a downright dislike. Because the cold I had caught en route to Portugal had become more congested, both Betty and our *Servita* were reluctant for me to go to the Basilica for the Invalids' Mass at 10 o'clock. I could override their protests, but as doing so hardly seemed fair to Betty, I begged the Blessed Mother to grant that I wouldn't have to surrender my ultimate goal after coming so far.

At two minutes to ten the rain stopped. Five minutes after, I was in the crowded Basilica where the pontifical Mass had just begun. At its conclusion, Bishop Marling of Kansas City began to bless the invalids whose cots and wheel chairs formed two long columns down the center of the church. As the Bishop moved along the line across from me I could see him raise the Monstrance above each afflicted person and hear the supplications: "Lord, make me well! . . . Lord, restore my sight! . . . O Lord, permit me to walk! . . . Heal me, Lord! . . . I believe in You! . . ."

Tears blinded me. I couldn't turn my head to see when my turn would come, but Betty's hand closed over mine as a signal. . . . Suddenly I felt a pulling sensation that withdrew me from the present and dissolved the crowd at either side.

I was in Galilee and coming toward me was the Son of God. . . . I had but to ask and He could cure me. . . .

My wise decision about a partial cure vanished completely. I was conscious only of Christ's power and a desperate longing that started from somewhere deep within me, pushed its way up my aching throat and through my lips with a pleading cry: "O DEAR GOD, IF IT IS YOUR HOLY WILL, MAKE ME WELL AGAIN! LET ME WALK AGAIN! PLEASE, DEAR GOD, PLEASE!"

I waited for the miracle to happen — waited for one time-suspended moment in which my future tottered on a threadline between health and helplessness. But that now-or-never moment passed me by, and so did the miracle. Regret ripped through me like a fiery sword, leaving a path of scalding tears.

Several agonizing moments later, I was filled with a sweet, indescribable peace and clarity that left no room for confusion. For suddenly I knew beyond all doubt that God wanted me to remain an invalid — a *complete invalid* — and that only through this physical imprisonment would I be led to eternal freedom. This was God's will, and all of me accepted the decision. But as this incomparable peace flowed into the soul of *Mary Ellen-invalid*, tears fell silently from *Mary Ellen-woman*, for in her heart a wake was being held for a dream that had just died.

CHAPTER 23

ALL THIS AND MARY TOO

FROM the train window I watched Fatima fade from sight. It had been difficult to say good-by to this sacred place and to the friends I met there. (If I had known that Fausto and Danny would be writing to me and that Vincent Goldstein and I would meet again — the next time in America — the parting would have been less sad.) Sixty hours earlier both the place and the people had been strangers. Now I was already missing them. This would have been virtually impossible in the States, for we are inhibited by the caution and distrust we pretend is convention. But in Fatima, where time is measured by love instead of seconds, this didn't seem strange at all.

I watched the unfamiliar plains hurrying past, gray and blurred under a deluge. The rain reminded me of the tears that had fallen that morning in Fatima as the Pilgrim Virgin statue was carried from the Basilica to the Apparition Chapel, its permanent resting place. The sunlit piazza, brushed by a rainbow that arched its feathery plumes above the eighty-thousand people, saw the crowd part to admit the procession of devout statue bearers, invalids, uniformed police from Dublin, and a long column of priests and religious who, with the Portuguese pilgrims, sang "Adeus, Noesa Senhora" (Good-by, our Lady).

Then Mary's image passed by with men and women waving white handkerchiefs and weeping openly. Why not? She is their mediator, inspiration, their comfort, their strength, their hope for tomorrow. After all, she is *their* Lady.

Soon the piazza grew silent. I could still feel the peace that descended, for it seemed to be made of all the prayers and sacrifices that had risen heavenward, been sifted through a veil and were being sprinkled softly upon the pilgrims below.

I returned to the Retreat-house with the seminarians while Betty and several of the wheelchair invalids were taken out to see the home of Ti and Marto, parents of Jacinta and Francisco. After the boys left, I talked with our *Servita,* who was so much a part of what I had just experienced. Interrupted by a soft knock at the door, she admitted the guests quickly, a look of surprise, recognition, and joy in her face. She spoke in Portuguese to them — an aged man and a woman of about forty — and greeted Michael Grace, the American with them.

"Mary Ellen," the latter said, coming toward me with the slight elderly man, "this is Ti Marto and his daughter. . . ."

The father of the children to whom our Lady appeared! I looked up into kind gray eyes that smiled at me as he bent over and kissed my hand. He wore a swooping mustache, a vested suit of considerable vintage, and an almost tangible cloak of humility that enveloped him from his saintly head to his poorly shod feet. I longed to speak his language, but when he said good-by, I felt sure that he understood what my heart wanted to say and my words could not express.

"Pray, Pray, Pray!" our Lady warned at Fatima. At Fatima, I had tried to do just that.

On our way to Lourdes the downpour raged for 20 hours and washed away so much of the railroad that the train had to stop while a single engine went ahead to test the track. Sometimes we waited for five hours before inching ahead another few miles. By 10 P.M. the diner was out of food. An hour later, we were told that our group would detrain and spend the night at a small hotel in Hendaye, Spain. The news suited me fine. A hotel meant food, and for breakfast I would order a steak . . . well done.

The delay in reaching Lourdes gave me a chance for long talks with George Gautier, one of our couriers. He reminded me of a nonmusical Maurice Chevalier. Unlike the French matinee idol, he was thin, only slightly graying, and less exhuberant. But like the man he resembled, he was charming and gracious, and was a raconteur *par excellence,* his expressive voice and dancing eyes bringing vivid credibility to the yarns he spun.

Conscripted at 18 into the English army during World War I,

he developed an abiding hatred of violence and destruction. He found employment later in France, married an English girl and to them a son and daughter were born. In the early 30's George went to work for a travel agency—as a guide during the tourist season, and a contact man the rest of the time. As he roamed Europe from his homeland to the Continent, George saw the wounds of war slowly heal. Then with terrorizing swiftness he heard the Hitler goose-step stomping its way across one country after another. Twenty-four hours before Paris fell, George heard that his wife, with other British subjects, had been placed in an internment camp. Still free himself, he tried desperately to persuade authorities to release his wife in exchange for his own surrender. The answer was an emphatic no.

For the next four years George Gautier walked the fields by day and slept in ditches at night. Physical suffering took its toll, but on this gentleman with the sensitivity of an artist and the soul of a recluse, the scars of those long tortured years are not the visible kind.

There was a poignant, almost haunting quality about him that clutched at my heart. I enjoyed talking with him, but I liked listening even better, for in each session he shared with me some of his thoughts, ideas born of quiet wisdom, patience, and charity. A realist by circumstances, a dreamer by nature, he regarded people with a paternal indulgence, wishing that they would change their ways, yet resigned that they would not. "We have developed into a race of automatons," he said one day. "We hurry to work, hurry to lunch, hurry back to work, hurry home, eat, fall asleep reading the paper, and then drag to bed so we can start all over again the next day! We have lost the art of communicating with one another. We have forgotten the joy of quiet meditation and have become afraid of being alone with ourselves and each other."

His words were never bitter, only a bit sad, as though life was a play he had already seen.

It surprised me that he wasn't a Catholic. His attentiveness at Mass and the ease with which he spoke of religious matters had left me thinking he was. My discovery led to a discussion of the many ingredients that go into living, especially faith. Hesitantly, even shyly, George admitted that he was "infatuated with the Lady Mary."

"Have you told her so?"

"I feel too unworthy — and yet I think she knows."

"But a woman likes to be told. Besides, the Devil often uses a sense of unworthiness as a wedge to keep us from coming close to Mary. You see he knows she'll try to lead that soul on to her Son."

"At Fatima, I finally lost the habit of thinking of her as someone to admire from a distance. I even talked to her — once as I would to a Queen, and once as a girl. . . ."

"And even as a Mother, *your* Mother?"

He shook his head. "Sometime, maybe. Perhaps at Lourdes. . . ."

Next morning, fortified by my breakfast of steak, I didn't mind when George told Betty and me that the six-hour ride to Lourdes was to be in the baggage car. For that decision I shall ever be grateful, partly because I could have seen very little from the compartment window, but mostly because I was given both time and the chance to prepare myself spiritually for the visit to another miraculous shrine.

Aware of my reactions at Fatima, George seemed to understand my conviction that if God had wanted to cure me, He would have done so there. But since I wasn't regarding Lourdes as another chance, what, if any, was my purpose in going there — other than its being a famed spot included on the itinerary?

Uneasiness tugged at me. Reluctant to part with what I experienced at the Portugal shrine, I had postponed serious thinking about the one in France. Now my French friend in whom the influence of Mary was already showing, wanted to know what I expected — or needed — from the Queen of Lourdes. At that moment all I wanted was the wisdom to choose the right words, for I longed to have this dear wanderer find a homecoming in the arms of our Lady, his Mother.

"You remember what I said about accepting God's will?"

He nodded his graying head.

"Well, my intellect accepts it, and most of the time my will does, but for those times it won't, I'm going to need help. And who can help me better than God's own Mother?"

"You mean you'll ask at Lourdes for — as you say — grace to live up to the truths you discovered at Fatima."

"Exactly. Only that isn't all. My career is one of illness and sacrifice. Just as in any other career, I can be successful, mediocre, or a flop. Naturally, I want the first — not only for the usual reasons — but because in this case success means my will being one with God's, and the more it is, the more God can work through me."

"That rather puts the reins back into your hands, doesn't it?"

"And how! When I remember that He used the likes of me to bring the League of Shut-Ins into being, I'm almost scared of what He might try to accomplish through me if I were a worthier instrument. As the priest told us at Lisieux, 'In God's hands Therese wanted to be as putty.' She was, too, and that's why she's *Saint* Therese!"

"Then you do have favors to ask the Lady at Lourdes, Mary Ellen."

"I do indeed, George. I want to beg for the repose of my father's soul, and that Mom will stay well and be spared to me for a long, long time, and for the graces my brother needs, and for relatives and all our shut-ins and benefactors, and for friends and priests and nuns I always pray for, and prisoners and missionaries. . . ."

His chuckle rose to a hearty laugh and I got the message.

"And for couriers!" I added quickly.

Never before had I been glad to ride in a baggage car. Once into the Pyrenees, one exquisite scene rapidly followed another. It reminded me of something St. Thomas Aquinas said about our having to relinquish one moment before we can take hold of the next one.

Shortly before George pointed out the spire of the Lourdes Basilica, we saw nestled among clusters of tall spruce, a circular lake — azure, opaque, and as calm as a sleeping kitten. Its backdrop of green trees would have formed a solid pattern except for red-roofed houses hugging the mountainside. Up still higher stood irregular peaks, and low above them a serpentine cloud crawled along slowly and then gracefully descended on their heads like a lacy shawl.

"What a fitting prelude to Mary's shrine!" I said to George as the spire of the Basilica now stood out in sharp detail against the sky.

We learned at the grotto the next day that the delay caused by heavy rains had prevented us from seeing the season's final candle-light procession. My disappointment wasn't intense, for before the smoke-blackened niche in which the Blessed Mother had appeared to Bernadette Soubirous, I found the same peace I had found at Fatima. It wasn't difficult to understand why. It emanated from the same immaculate source.

To an invalid who has prayed for a cure before the Lourdes shrine, it must seem strange that I do not regard this stop the major high light of my journey. For Dixie, Dorothy, and Irene, the stretcher cases who didn't go to Fatima, Lourdes contained all the pomp, ceremony, suspense, and spiritual enrichment they had hoped for. If I had stayed at Lourdes, I'm sure it would have been all this to me, too. But I had gone first to Fatima, and for me it was a place and an experience not to be equaled. As Fatima was unique; so, in its own way, was Lourdes. For there I had time to take stock of myself and give my friendship with the Mother of God a chance to grow.

On our last day at Lourdes, rain shortened our time at the grotto. The drivers quickly loaded the wheel chair and stretcher travelers into the chartered bus. When my turn came, there was no room. I assured them I didn't mind. In spite of the rain, I welcomed the opportunity to have some time alone at the shrine.

Since our Lady's apparition in 1858, people from all over the world have been coming here, some out of curiosity, but most of them to seek favors from her. My heart suddenly filled with sadness for those who didn't know her or who regarded her as remote and unapproachable.

She is gentle as a sigh, mighty as a roar, tantalizing as spring. She is unique among all creatures, having been kept free from sin from the instant of her conception. She embodies all that is regal, rare, and radiant; yet she walks in humility. *She is the Queen of*

Saints and the refuge of sinners. Understanding, too, is hers (remember how thoughtfully she prevented embarrassment at the wedding in Cana by telling her Son the wine was gone?), and faith (and how she commanded the stewards to fill the wine jugs with water?), and consideration (did she not make a tiresome journey to visit an aged cousin while she was with child?), and compassion (was she not the beloved friend of the Magdalen whose tears once washed the feet of Christ?).

Mary is all these things and more. . . . She is a defense attorney, go-between, counselor, comforter, guide. She is a Woman who has known love, loneliness, anxiety, heartbreak, poverty, rebuke, fear, and the sharp thrusts of gossip. . . . She is a Woman wrapped in silence and veiled in obscurity. . . . A cameo-lovely Sovereign with love in her eyes and grace at her finger tips. . . . Most of all she is a Mother, not of one Man alone, but to every man everywhere.

To those who give themselves to Mary, she gives herself in return. Among those who do not, there are some who believe that too much honor goes to Mary. Their ignorance is to be pitied, not condemned; for they are blind to the fact that she keeps nothing, wants nothing, for herself. She is no more an obstacle between Christ and us than a window pane is to the sun. She is instead a sieve through which our good acts, prayers, and sufferings are filtered and refined before being presented to Christ. If all of them were given to Him with their original imperfections, I'm afraid there would be a lot of rejects.

In souls totally dedicated to her she works wonders. Eagerly, tenderly, she prepares them for a veritable assault of divine love and obtains for them the courage to persevere . . . to trust . . . to surrender to God's wishes and, one day, to embrace eternal life.

She is the one person who, because God willed it so, was necessary to Him. A virgin, she brought forth a Child in a cave that sheltered beasts of burden. As heaven bent low to adore the Word made Flesh, her heart shed tears of mixed joy and pain. For there, cradled in straw, was not just her Baby, but the long awaited Messias! Time would rob her of the Son nestled against her, and time would keep reminding her that only this tragedy would reopen the gates of heaven.

Mary is love fashioned into a Woman; Purity garbed in sandals and a blue mantle; Gentleness holding the world in one hand and the Infant in the other. Her words are music, her touch velvet, her power an atomic force. . . . She is an aqueduct through which Christ came to us. . . . She is my gateway to Paradise.

A moment before the bus returned, I noticed a man kneeling at the grotto. He was all alone. I squinted my myopic eyes and peered through the rain. The solitary figure was George Gautier. No candles flickered, no ceremony relieved the stark grayness of the historic cove, no hymns sang a counter melody to the pelting rain. And yet something held this man here, something kept him from hurrying to the nearest shelter. . . .

I knew then what our Fatima *Servita* meant when she said, "The greatest miracles are the miracles of grace." My tears of joy mixed with the raindrops on my face as I asked our Lady to bless the man kneeling at her feet.

CHAPTER 24

I CAME, I SAW, I WEPT

"PALM trees in Nice?" I asked in surprise.

"*Mais oui!*" replied the petite volunteer wearing the *Croix Rouge* armband. With a smile she loosed a ripple of melodic tones that might have carried a lovely message if I had understood French. It served me right for greeting her with "*Il fait beau aujourd 'hui!*" the one sentence I could *parley-vous.*

Dearly as I loved the simplicity of Fatima and the makeshift (though pleasant) accommodations at Lourdes, the luxury of the Nice hotel temporarily lulled my concern for spiritual advancement. Roses from Janet Muth brightened our room, and four-course dinners brightened my disposition. For the first time in four weeks I abandoned my cot and slept in a bed, every bone in my body breathing out relief as I sank into inner-spring bliss. Betty had her hair set in a salon; then she shampooed mine as I lay cornerwise on the bed and hung my head over a portable plastic tub.

Refreshed and refueled, we were jubilant to learn that our first sidetrip would be Monte Carlo. As soon as my cot was securely blocked and tied, I settled down for a restful drive. But I underestimated the Grand Corniche road, one built by the Romans long before Nero fiddled his first tune. High up in the mountains, the road pirouetted like a prima ballerina. Once again my heart thumped as I looked out the window and down the rugged slopes.

Empty fortresses built to repel invaders stared back at us through hollow eyes. They spoke of a tyranny whose greed was its own destruction. More modern signs of a later tyranny were remnants of Nazi road blocks, now mute testimony of a madman's dream.

The bus stopped abruptly. "There," said the driver, pointing down to a neck of land that jetted out into a body of incredibly blue water, "is Monte Carlo!"

I wondered how we could get from our lofty vantage point to the spot he pointed out below, but, after a few more turns, we entered the capital city of Monaco. We skirted the famed casino, window-shopped, bought post cards and drove through the grounds of the ducal palace. Little did I know that a few years later another Kelly girl would be getting a much warmer reception.

We returned to Nice along the seashore route. Caught in the embrace of sunset, the Mediterranean resisted for a while, then surrendered its blue to the eclipsing advances of the enraptured pursuer. Darkness swiftly dropped its curtain on their union, leaving us with but a memory of a blue sea and a Riviera sunset.

Five hundred miles and sixty-eight tunnels later we eased into Rome's ultramodern station. It was exactly midnight. Tired clear to my toes, I closed my eyes for another "squeeze play" through the train window and wished they could stay closed. We were met by ten *Charitas*, a group of businessmen and students who aid afflicted travelers without charge and often at the expense of a day's wages. They were extremely kind, but none spoke English — a fact which led to complications.

As the volunteers assisted the other invalids off the train, I wondered how I could explain to them that they would not have to carry me to the bus if they put the wheels back on my cot. Oh well, I thought, George Gautier will be back any time now, and it shouldn't take Betty too long to check up on our luggage. But at that moment the men converged around my cot, picked me up, exchanged a flurry of words and put me down. I saw one of them point to the wheels lying on the cement platform. Thank goodness! I whispered; now we'll have no trouble at all. Then I remembered that the rear wheels were without ball bearings, and if the men took one wheel with bearings and one without for a pair, my cot would behave like a donkey.

I couldn't move my head to nod a "yes, use the wheels," and of course I couldn't gesture, but since there was a chance of their getting them on right, I said "Yes." But when I saw a man start to put two unmatched wheels on the foot end of my cot, I shouted "No!" My confused helpers dropped the wheels like hot potatoes, picked me up and started once more up the long terminal.

Scarcely five minutes later these willing volunteers stopped, put me down, mopped their brows and scooped me up again. I heard a rumbling noise from behind and saw a strange-looking four-sided baggage cart stop beside us. A bit of handwaving conveyed the message; again I replied, "Yes" — yes, I would go in the cart, though my feet would be higher than my head. I suddenly recalled a song recorded by Ezio Pinza. I didn't have the vaguest idea of its meaning, only that it was Italian and gay. So without further rhyme or reason I hollered with tired but happy gusto, "ANDIAMO!"

I didn't know why the *Charitas* stared at me and took off with the cart in a burst of laughter. The next day I learned that "Andiamo" meant "Let's get going!"

Once again we were quartered in a hospital — Salvator Mundi — but, unlike the one in Paris, this beautiful international clinic did much to make my six days in Rome something to remember. Nearly every morning we were loaded into the bus by the *Charitas* who crowded our days with the expertness of sardine packers. We saw Victor Emmanuel Square, the Roman Forum and Colosseum, moss-draped remains of Nero's palace, the American Embassy, and swank apartment houses done in "shocking pink."

We saw St. Callistus' Catacombs — for centuries the headquarters of the world's most courageous underground — the Arc of Titus, Venezzia Square, and Plazza del Populo. Of the Basilicas we saw, St. Paul's Outside-The-Walls was my favorite. St. Peter's, of course, has no equal. I won't attempt to describe either St. Peter's or my reactions to it. I know my limitations.

I had an extra reason to be happy in Rome in addition to the usual pleasure of touring. The La Salette Missionaries were there. Several scholastics I had known at Ipswich, Mass., and near Iowa's Lake Okoboji, were attending this major seminary, and the superior of the American Brothers (the Rome house of studies has boys from Switzerland, France, Poland, and the U. S.) was also a dear friend. Seeing them at any time is a profound joy, but this meeting in a foreign country had a satisfaction all its own. As far as I was concerned, Rome's guidebooks were inadequate regarding the city's wonders. For me they existed wherever the La Salettes hung their hats.

Our audience with the Holy Father was to be held at Castel Gandolfo, where, Father Cahill told us, we would be able to see him for a much longer time than in Rome.

The buses arrived to take us to the summer home of His Holiness, situated in the Alban Hills, some 20 miles from the City. Seeing this great man was all that mattered — especially since his poor health had caused the cancellation of audiences up until a short time earlier. The ride over, we were carried through the gateway of a high brick wall and into a large cobblestone courtyard only sparsely filled. Tall Swiss guards in colorful uniforms were sprinkled throughout the circular enclosure. Plain clothesmen checked to see that there were no cameras or concealed boxes. An hour later, this piazza was jammed.

The tension became electric. A black cloud rolled overhead and disapproving murmurs arose from the crowd. Seconds later, as if it had overheard the threats from below, the ominous intruder moved on. Silent again, we watched and waited, some two thousand of us — the invalids placed in the front line, the others behind.

A light in the balcony window brought a deafening cheer from the waiting crowd. The cheers increased as a papal chamberlain hung a red tapestry from the balcony ledge, and grew louder . . . louder. . . .

And then he appeared — *the Vicar of Christ!* I stared up at him, my heart thumping above the crowd's roar. Immaculate in white, he stood there with the dignity of a king and the humility of a peasant, his lean face smiling slightly, his arms uplifted, as though giving to God the demonstration accorded him. He seemed carved from marble, his features chiseled and worn with age. In dramatic contrast to his motionless frame, his piercing brown eyes blazed like twin fires.

The moment he spoke, the exultant cries shrank to a whisper, then silence. In six languages he delivered his messages, each group responding jubilantly to the sound of its native tongue. While addressing the Italian members of the crowd, the Holy Father laughed aloud as a question from below broke a moment of silence. He answered it quickly, apparently to the amusement of all who understood. When he spoke in English, I strained to hear every word. For those that followed, I was totally unprepared:

"We are happy to extend a very special welcome to the First National Pilgrimage of Invalids to the Shrines of Europe, sponsored by the Confraternity of Pilgrims in the United States of America. In particular it is a great joy to Us to greet those of you who have endured great sacrifice, and even pain, to come from your homes thousands of miles away on a long and difficult journey in order to visit the Vicar of Christ.

"We know that you are members of the League of Shut-In Sodalists, which was founded largely through the persevering efforts of one of you, Our beloved daughter, Mary Ellen Kelly. . . ."

A numbness came over me. I stared up at the man on the balcony with a strange feeling of unreality: *this just couldn't be happening to me!* Then I heard him ask: "Which is she?" and he leaned forward, waiting for me to be pointed out. A man standing behind my cot obliged. The Holy Father looked directly at me and smiled. My spirits soared higher than before and I could feel my soul smiling back.

"We are sure that your visit to the sacred shrines and the Eternal City has given you a new courage and strength to bear the sufferings that God has been pleased to ask of you.

"You are especially dear to the heart of Our Divine Master, to His Blessed Mother, and also to Us, for with Saint Paul, We may say to You: 'The grace that has been granted to you is that of suffering for Christ's sake, not merely believing in Him.' Treasure this suffering that is yours through God's will; bear it always in union with Our suffering Lord, offering it to Him for the increase and sanctification of the members of His Body. Thus you will help to 'Fill up the sufferings of Christ . . . for His Body, which is the Church.' In the words of Saint Peter, the first Vicar of Christ, We exhort you: 'Do not be surprised, beloved, that this fiery ordeal should have befallen you, to test your quality; there is nothing strange in what is happening to you. Rather rejoice, when you share in some measure the sufferings of Christ; so joy will be yours, and triumph, when His glory is revealed.'

"Carry this message of Ours back to all the other members of your Sodality and League of Shut-In Sodalists who couldn't make this pilgrimage with you. And now, in a very special way and with all Our Heart, We bless you and them, and all your loved ones, as well as all those who have helped to make this pilgrimage possible and all those who have come with you."

The Holy Father remained on the balcony, giving His blessing to the crowd which expressed its love and homage with waving arms and cries of "*Viva il papa!*" I expressed mine the only way I could — by crying. I thought of a postal card sent to me during Holy Year from a friend who had just come from a papal audience. He quoted a phrase taken from the words of Simeon when he first beheld the Infant Christ: "Now thou canst dismiss Thy Servant, O Lord!" As the balcony door closed, removing from view the blessed sight of the Sovereign Pontiff, I repeated these words; for I knew, as did Simeon, that my heart would never again witness a more triumphant moment.

CHAPTER 25

WHAT, SO SOON?

ONLY ten days left in Europe! Milan's high lights were its immense "Cathedral of a Thousand Spires" and the bomb-ridden building that houses Da Vinci's fresco, *The Last Supper*. I didn't care much for the site of Mussolini's capture and execution. When we left Italy through an eleven mile tunnel, orange trees were golden with fruit; when we emerged some twenty dark minutes later, we saw snow-topped roofs against a background of white mountain peaks. I didn't need to be told this was Switzerland.

The days in Lucerne were like a prolonged Christmas. The crisp air gave us ravenous appetites and the tasty food at the Hotel Ritz-Carleton satisfied them completely. Our couriers had considered the streets of Paris and Rome hazardous for invalids, but Lucerne was an invalid shopper's paradise. My prized purchases were a wool shawl for Mother and three pairs of bright socks for Arie, the ship's carpenter. And especially precious to me is a souvenir gift from a shopkeeper — a little Swiss clock that hangs on the wall opposite my bed. I lost the key, so it doesn't run. But I don't care. Sometimes it's rather comforting to see time stand still.

On the morning of our trip to Einsiedeln, where the Church of the Benedictines was consecrated in 948, Betty and I watched from the bus window for a glimpse of my cousin, Jerry Ronan, 27, a civilian employee with the army in Austria. We hadn't met for twenty years, so the Lucerne reunion promised to be a gala one. With split-second timing he arrived, his black curly hair tousled, his dark eyes snapping with excitement.

"Hurry!" I shouted. "We're all ready to leave for Einsiedeln for the day. Pile aboard!" He had to sit in front of us all the way but

I didn't object. It isn't every day one comes across a cousin who looks handsome from the back.

Though he had seen most of Europe's wonders, Jerry shared our fascination with Mt. Pilatus from which, according to legend, Pontius Pilate committed suicide after condemning Christ to die. On the crest of the mountain is a striking outline of a man with a decided Roman nose and tunic. This, says legend, is Pilate, whose spirit was raised from the sea below and sentenced by God to be forever imprisoned within the granite image of himself.

The following day I was looking at Pilatus from our balcony when I heard a strange noise. I tried my best to identify the whispering sound, but couldn't. When George Gautier joined me later, I asked, "What in the world is that noise, George? Listen. . . ."

"Why that's the falling leaves," he replied after a moment. "It is their song of farewell to their mother." He walked toward a large tree whose branches brushed our balcony. "One should never intercept a leaf in its descent," he went on softly, "because the mother listens until she hears her leaves safely reach the ground. Then and only then is she assured that their life's cycle has been completed."

I'll also cling to the memory of our last evening in Switzerland. To entertain us, the hotel engaged a troupe of local musicians and dancers headed by a one-man circus named Franz Hug (it sounded like hook). Years earlier he had come to America to appear in a Laurel and Hardy comedy, "The Swiss Miss." Together the group whooped and hollered, waved flags, danced, played spoons, yodeled, blew Alpine horns, and sang their way right into our hearts. I remember the happiness reflected in the faces of Janet Muth, Dixie MacMaster, the afflicted nuns, and our other disabled travelers. Soon they would be home, back once more in the restricted routine which would never be the same again. But that night the enchantment still enveloped them and they wore it like an original creation.

The next day at the station I tried to hold back the tears when Jerry and the volunteer helpers said good-by. Like the beauty slipping past me, my time with Jerry slipped through my finger tips. I had tried to hold on, but even as the tears fell, the land of William Tell was already far behind me.

Brussels sparkled with friendly excitement. Comfortably quartered at the Hotel Metropole, we took advantage of the adjoining arcade and shopped until either our funds or cot pushers were exhausted. Betty and George, my bargain-hunting companions, deserve an award for venturing beyond the arcade, smooth, sheltered, and stepless, onto the sloping streets.

"George, can't you keep your end of the cot over a little more?" Betty would ask in slightly edgy tones.

"I believe it's your end that's causing the trouble," George would answer, implying that no more could be expected from a woman pusher.

I promised to call it a day as soon as I had bought one more gift for a friend and a hat for myself. This sounded reasonable, so we started up a side street in search of a moderately priced hat shop. As usual, I ended up in a lavish *chapelier* where I fell hook, line, and sinker for a little black number that George endorsed with full masculine approval. The gift I later selected was a copper pitcher.

"You'll never get that in your suitcase," Betty warned.

"Oh well, I can always carry it on the cot between my feet. . . ." It was still there when I left the ship, along with two dozen tulip bulbs, a tea pot from Milan, and a box containing my most valuable possession: the Holy Father's cap — his pontifical *zucchetto*.

Two days of rain failed to dampen my enthusiasm over Holland, this clean, fresh country — land of dikes, windmills, tulips, canals, and wonderful people. Amsterdam, Rotterdam, Alsmeer, Volendam, and the Hague — each with its own personality, yet all sharing a symmetry of pattern, purpose, and spirit. I loved the cities; the country; the neat scrubbed houses and slender canals running parallel with the front door thresholds; vast beds of tulips that nodded their colorful heads as we passed by. I loved the people we met — waiters, bellboys, elevator operators, our bearded guide, and a young man from Rotterdam with whom I had corresponded. Like my friends from the ship's crew, they struck me as having strength, pride, and durability.

It was easy to picture them here: Arie skating across a pond in long, effortless strides; Kees listening to his beloved music; Rita getting ready for a date; and Hank sitting on the step of his mother's house. Suddenly I was lonely for them. "Please let them be on the ship," I prayed.

We boarded the *Nieuw Amsterdam* the morning of November 6. The ride to Rotterdam had been pleasant, but my heart wasn't in it. Now on the ship I realized for the first time that I had left myself scattered all over Europe. George Gautier pushed my cot into the main lounge, which I recognized as the one in which we'd first met.

"This is where I get off, Mary," I heard him say behind me. I couldn't answer. He came forward and I looked into his dear face, sad and drawn in the sunless light. The moment I had avoided thinking about was here. Without mercy it crowded against me, squeezing hot tears into my eyes. He bent down and kissed me. The words to express my gratitude and affection wouldn't come. All I could say was, "Good-by, George."

My enchanted floating kingdom gave its passengers a rough time on the return crossing. One day the ship's paper reported 40-foot waves at Hoboken — an item that sent a fourth of my co-travelers to bed and another fourth to the nearest railing. But my world was steady and sun-filled, for my prayers were answered. Rita, Kees, Arie, and Hank were aboard.

I would enjoy recreating the happy memories of that voyage, but, in behalf of every invalid in the United States who would like to travel and can't, I want instead to direct a protest to owners of our nation's railroads. "Why isn't there at least one coach car equipped to accommodate stretcher passengers?"

In the thousands of miles I have traveled, some 3700 of them have been in a baggage car. There are three reasons for this: I couldn't afford to go first class, or the windows of the train were too small for my cot to pass through, or they were hermetically sealed. If someone in my condition could be lifted into a berth, the cost would be less; since this is impossible, the extra charge of a bedroom, roomette, or drawing room is unavoidable. Because most invalid travelers need assistance, the additional expense of the attendant's fare boosts the total sky high.

A fancy coach wouldn't be necessary, only one that would admit a wheel chair or stretcher through its door and had facilities to hold it securely beside a window. A supply of blankets and pillows would prove helpful (the Swiss cars had them), and an overhead U-shaped rod equipped with a draw drape could provide a private cubicle.

Past discussions on this subject have usually raised the question of there being too few of the afflicted to warrant such a coach. On a full-time basis, yes, but why couldn't summer schedules be set up just as excursion trains are added? If they were planned to avoid busy periods, e.g., the closing and beginning of school, holidays and conventions, I can't see what great problems would arise. From the potential number of crippled passengers, through letters, direct conversation and thoughts expressed to me, I am convinced that the number would be surprising.

It is also likely to increase steadily. Think of the thousands of men and women whose active lives have been altered by polio, multiple sclerosis, arthritis, cerebral palsy, accidents, and wars. To these, add all the congenitally disabled and the aged who, though young in heart, conserve their strength by semi-confinement in a wheel chair. With the right accommodations we could break away from sameness by visiting relatives and friends; we could vacation at a resort or lodge, see some shows, attend a few ball games, reunions, religious functions, or just enjoy the change of scenery. If we could do this without fear of falling, getting dirty from head to toe, hurting our feet, bruising our hands against unyielding windows, causing extra commotion and work, feeling like a gold fish, or ending up in debt for years, we would be accomplishing another abolition of slavery — this time one freeing the physically handicapped.

Betty and I were the last ones to leave the *Nieuw Amsterdam* the morning we disembarked. Arie, who had made a handsome sewing cabinet for Mother during the crossing, had accepted my invitation to join us for dinner that evening in New York. Kees promised to be with him. I'd said good-by to Hank, but this was not my last good-by to Rita. She went through customs with me; then abruptly, we reached the end of the line. I was lifted quickly into the station wagon and watched her from there until the crowd blocked her from my view. I prayed that neither the ocean, nor time nor distance would weaken the bond between us.

Hours later in the hotel, good-by's were said once more. As Kees and Arie were closing the door, a hall draft pulled it from their hands. That door's slam didn't jar me physically, but it released the brakes on my heart with such a jolt that all its postponed hurts, concealed disappointments, and unfulfilled dreams tumbled forth. For them I cried . . . and for the dear friends who would be ever separated from me by an ocean . . . over stored-up sadness, unadmitted insecurities . . . for the feeling that I had failed those who had made the journey possible . . . and I cried over the shattered picture I had of myself walking down the gangplank, embracing Mother, strolling up Main Street in Marcus. . . .

From a deep well of confusion and self-pity, my tears kept falling onto these crumbled defenses and broken dreams until the New York skyline gave its first hint of dawn.

CHAPTER 26

LETTER TO AN INVALID

My dear friend:

Your letter was the most heart-warming and provoking one I've received in a long time. I wish our beds were close together so that we could talk (by the way, you most certainly may call me Kelly — all my friends do!). But since many miles separate us, I might as well dispense with the amenities and get right down to business.

In reference to our exchange of thoughts on contemplation, you asked me if you are being presumptuous in hoping that you'll be led to this lofty state. How often I wondered the same thing! For a long time I was afraid that I was being presumptuous. Then finally I realized that this doubt was merely an excuse to justify my laxity. Humility is a fine thing, but don't be deceived by a false substitute. The only way to acquire humility is to be humbled, so that there's no need to be afraid of the consequences. Maybe you'll fall flat on your big intentions, but perhaps that will be God's way of giving you new strength to start again with more trust in Him.

The other night I read a magnificent article about contemplation by Father Michael of the Holy Family, O.C.D. Since then I have been longing to discuss the subject with someone, and although the joy of doing so face to face would be greater, I'm glad for the chance to share my thoughts with someone like you — someone vitally interested.

First of all, does the word "contemplation" frighten you? Does it seem too advanced, too ambitious for you and me? With every day that passes I become more convinced that it is not. What exactly is it, you ask? According to St. John of the Cross, it is "an infused and loving knowledge of God which enlightens the soul and enkindles it until it is raised up step by step even unto God its Creator." St. Thomas Aquinas says that this process "consists chiefly in the contemplation of God, of which charity is the motive." In it is delight, "not only because of the contemplation itself, but also by reason of the Divine love. In both respects the delight thereof surpasses all human delight, both because spiritual delight is greater than carnal pleasure, and because the love whereby God is loved out of charity surpasses all love."

If contemplation and its rewards are so desirable, one wonders why so few reach this high spiritual plane. In the *Living Flame of Love* by St. John of the Cross, Father Michael finds the answer: "It is clear . . . that the chief reason is the lack of generosity and co-operation on the part of the soul, and that God would desire to grant contemplation to all."

A lack of generosity. . . . Is it really as simple as that? Does it all boil down to our stinginess with God? It seems incredible! Yet, as I have thought it over, this lack of generosity explains many imperfections the source of which I have never before pinpointed. We are generous with God when it pleases us — even more so when we want a favor. But what a howl we put up each time He asks us to let go of something we want to hold onto!

And why? Because we love that something more than we love Him. There are times, thank goodness, when we comply with most of His requests humbly and without too much protest. But sooner or later self-love creeps in and usurps the love that belongs to God. Then docility changes quickly to ego-centered determination.

It is this "I" in us that makes us say cruel, cutting words when we are annoyed, that keeps us from accepting false accusations silently, and demands vindication for ruffled pride. It is the "I" in us that likes flattery and is quick to rationalize our faults.

It leads us to expect compensations for every physical trial as though we were special. Because of it we want comfort, understanding, and encouragement, not in a moderate dosage, but in greedy, "king-size" amounts.

You remarked that forgetting self must be easier for nuns. I thought that once, too. They've got it made, I used to tell myself.

Their surrender is complete, so it must be easy for them to be generous with God. It's as though — well — as though they have nothing to lose. After all, since they've already given up everything and consecrated themselves to God, there shouldn't be too much left to keep them from achieving perfection. But why, I then wondered, aren't all nuns saints? The answer is simply expressed in a salient bit from the *Imitation of Christ:* "*. . . all men are frail but you must admit that none is more frail than yourself.*"

How easy it had been for me to forget that nuns are human beings and therefore subject to the effects of original sin. Each time the memory of my foolish question came back to mind, I said to myself sternly, "Are you dumb!" Did I think that their vows made them strangers to the doubts and rebellions that sooner or later sneak into every human heart? Everyone must fight his own spiritual battles, I reminded myself, and the closer a soul comes to God, the harder Satan works to conquer it.

In spite of my realizing these facts (I am ashamed to admit this), I still couldn't completely rid my mind of the idea that attaining the contemplative life ought to be at least easier for nuns and priests. Then from nowhere came a question that looked me square in the eye and demanded: "And how about applying the same principle to people like yourself — to *total invalids?* You've given up almost everything, haven't you? Then why do you still hold back? Why do you remain only a partial giver? Why don't you attain perfection? What do you have to lose?"

Me attain perfection?

As if the voice asked "Why not?" I began comparing my life with that of a religious.

It's true, I admitted cautiously, that each of us has given up a great deal. But my surrender was physical; the nun's, spiritual.

"So what?" the other voice seemed to say. "Your choice of accepting it willingly or with bitterness was certainly of a spiritual nature."

Yes, but the nun didn't have to accept God's call. I had no alternative: God tapped her on the shoulder, but He sent me a subpoena!

"All the more reason for you to work toward an intimate union with Christ! Since He didn't give you even a chance to get away, He proved that He wanted you and wouldn't take 'No' for an answer."

At this point, my dear friend, a great weariness enveloped me. It was useless to try to talk myself out of this. I had no excuse, and I knew it. God had indeed chosen me for Himself, wanting me to reach Him through the vocation of suffering. With my bed as a cloister, my improvised blouses and assorted sheets as my habit, and my stiff joints as binding vows, I had been called to serve Him — even to a spiritual sacrifice which would make my physical ones pale in comparison.

Then why aren't all invalids saints? I argued once more. What've we got to lose?

From all directions the answers to this question came at me, and loudest were the words which had started it all — Father Michael's quotation from St. John of the Cross: "It must be known that it is not because God is pleased that there should be few raised to this high spiritual state, for it would rather please Him that all souls should be perfect; but it is rather that He finds few vessels which can bear so high and lofty a work. . . . It is clear in this text that the chief reason is the *lack of generosity*. . . ."

This mental tug of war has brought into sharp focus the waste in the lives of people like you and me. Whether or not our first surrender was voluntary is not pertinent; the main thing is that we are entirely dependent upon God and, as there can be no doubt of a wrong career since He Himself chose it for us, our invalidism is our chance to obey His will to the letter.

We are even spared the uncertainty of wondering, "Is this what God wants of me?" Our work is laid out for us, the pattern is cut, our tools, forged in the burning love of our dying Saviour, are for the taking. Even a guide, His Mother, is standing by.

What a setup! Having already given up our plans, our dreams, and the freedom to move about, we have nothing to lose and everything to gain. Yet even we, still proud and self-centered in our beds and wheel chairs, are reluctant to GIVE ALL.

What is left to give?

All the self that remains in us, my dear friend; the self that dreams of what might have been and still reaches out for joys that are denied, that still pleads for respite, that rejects solitude, craves human praise and affection, and regards distractions and frequent distaste for prayer as sure signs that "the spiritual life is not for me. . . ." Let's be honest. Our willingness to suffer should be motivated not by the thought of eternal reward and temporal compensations, but by the clear truth that suffering is a golden opportunity and, for us, a basic duty.

Because of our inherent lack of generosity, the spiritual climb is hard to make. Decreasing this lack is hard, too. How can it be accomplished? That's a good question!

The first step, this would-be climber has learned, is to know himself. In case you haven't tried this, it's quite a trick. A story I heard on the radio illustrates my point. One day while walking along a road, a man saw a shiny object and picked it up. Not knowing that it was a mirror, he looked into the glass and said, "Well, whaddeya know — a photograph of my grandfather when he was younger! — and what a sorry-looking gent he was!" Later that day the man's wife discovered the mirror in her husband's pocket. Looking into the strange object she exclaimed heatedly, "Ah ha! So that's the old crony he's been running around with!"

"Know thyself," St. Augustine tells us. But it isn't easy to be honest with ourselves, doing away with all delusions, artifices, and excuses. It means assuming our responsibilities and admitting our unworthiness before and utter dependence upon God. Whoever accomplishes this task deserves the Celestial Medal of Honor, because the discovery that we aren't the noble attractive persons we thought we were takes courage. In fact, it knocks one's ego for a loop.

This cleansing of self is only the beginning. On the authority of our Lord Himself, it is an elementary process in the purgative way, an essential condition for those who would "see God." Now we are urged by spiritual writers to concentrate on knowing God, for if we wish to become united with Him, we must first know Him. This doesn't seem too difficult. After all, we already know quite a lot about Him: *The Supreme Spirit, who alone exists of Himself, and is infinite in all perfections . . . the first cause uncaused. . . . Three Divine Persons in One God — co-equal, co-eternal. . . .* Yes, we know these things about God and we can name His attributes as readily now as we did years ago in catechism class.

But is this knowing God? Not well enough. If we knew Him better, we couldn't offend Him so often or so grievously because, as the saints tell us, to know Him is to love Him, for nowhere is there anyone so completely perfect, so completely desirable.

Remember the popular Broadway musical, "The King and I"? One of its tunes was called *Getting to Know You,* and the words went something like this: "Getting to know you, getting to know more about you. . . . Getting to like you, hoping that you like me. . . ." This song made a lot of dollars; also a lot of sense. Haven't you often heard someone say, "Mrs. Jones? Yes, we're good friends. I used to think she was a snob, but once I got to know her. . . ." And who are your best friends? The people you know best, of course.

It follows, then, that the more intimate we become with these three Divine Persons who are God, the more we will come to love Them, and, consequently, try to avoid displeasing Them.

If we wished to know someone better — say a great and famous figure — we would read everything we could find about him, especially the works of authors who knew and loved him personally. We would want to spend more time with him. If he graciously suggested a specific hour each day for the meetings, we would get there on time and never miss an appointment without reason.

As our knowledge of this person increased, our appreciation of his ability, character, and wisdom would also increase. Result: we would seek ways to please this person whom we were learning to love and revere more and more.

This same process, the saints tell us, enables us to know God better (and can you think of a greater Personage?). First of all, we have at hand the works of His biographers — Matthew, Mark, Luke, and John. These men, whose admission into the fourth estate came unsolicited, may never have qualified for the Nobel Prize for Literature; yet their work has remained one of the world's best sellers since the invention of the printing press. No writers in history were as inspired or as capable of recording the life of a great man with as much objectivity, perception, clarity, and love.

Through the divine co-operation of the Godhead, an amazing plan of God brings Him close to us that we may know Him better. . . . This is activated in the unique drama of the Holy Sacrifice of the Mass, one that continues every hour of every day around the entire world. Its uniqueness lives in three facts: it is an autobiography of Love Incarnate co-authored by three Persons; it is a tragedy that has a happy ending, and regardless of the number of times it is re-enacted, repetition never palls: each performance is as new, fresh, and exciting as a premiere.

An additional distinction is the striking fact that neither the receptivity of the audience nor the experience of the performers changes the value of this timeless drama.

With this gradual conquest of self there evolves an almost indiscernible decrease of ego and, within the soul, an increase of Christ. As He is allowed more and more freedom in our spiritual tabernacles, our distaste for sin should grow keener and our interests and energies directed more and more toward God alone. In a word, our aim is to realize with St. Paul: "I live now not I, but Christ in me."

You asked me to recommend some books that would help us communicate with God. Among many excellent ones are *The Primer of Prayer*, by James McSorley, O.P., *True Devotion to the B.V.M.*, by St. Louis de Montfort, *Introduction to the Devout Life*, by St. Francis de Sales, and *The Imitation of Christ*, by St. Thomas à Kempis, and *Difficulties in Mental Prayer*, by Eugene Boylan, O.Cist.R.

And then we have the Blessed Mother, who is ever standing by, eager to lead another soul closer to God. With faithful daily effort and her help, we can pass through what spiritual writers term the "purgative way" and, with our spirits strengthened, reach that plane of contemplation wherein the soul begins to long for God and dwell upon His ineffable beauty. As the announcers of television's quiz shows would say, "You've reached the second plateau now.

The higher the stakes, the harder the questions." We don't have to worry, though. Mary knows how much God wants this kind of love from us and, by miracles of grace, will fortify the souls of those generous enough not to turn away.

Remember this passage in *The Way of Divine Love?* — "Yes, Josefa," Christ said to the young nun one day, "All I ask of souls is their love, but they give Me only ingratitude. . . . I call them and they turn away from Me. . . ."

Yes, as you said, some people are wrong in thinking that contemplation is only a temporary leave of absence from reality during which nothing is seen, heard, or felt. St. Thomas Aquinas says that man ought to see many things in contemplation — his sins, the punishments of hell, the promise of heaven, the desires of Christ, his neighbor's needs. Then we will find where the "manna" is found . . . that spiritual sweetness that so tantalizes the soul.

A tedious ascent? For me it gets so wearisome that at times I wish I could fly away through space until I landed right at God's feet. But there is no such rapid or easy transportation for the spiritual climb. It is beset by obstacles of our own making — our self-love, our petty faults.

Sometimes at night (thank God, it doesn't happen often) I long to turn on my side. My muscles strain as I try to change my position, but my arms and legs mock me with their very unmovingness. . . . I think of the years already spent on my back, the uncertain years ahead when I will still be helpless, unable to turn. The weight of the darkness, aloneness, and this bleak outlook crushes down on me. . . .

Sometimes I want to scream. Sometimes I cry. At other times I gather the strength to rout my tears with a stern rebuke: "You big baby! What a sorry companion you've turned out to be — whimpering, lying here in the dark, licking your wounds! What about our Lord? He couldn't move either, and under His bruised flesh there was hard wood instead of a soft mattress. So offer our Lady your suffering. And be thankful this cross was sent to you out of love, not punishment."

This is an example of an everyday encounter along my journey heavenward. Perhaps during the day I overcome some spiritual obstacle; that same night I might land face down in the rubble of self-indulgence.

For every step I take upward, I slide back four in spite of a voice within me that says, "Hold on, Kelly! Trust Him! Don't be afraid! Let Him lift you up . . . higher . . . higher. . . . Be generous. Be loyal. Be His TRUE LOVE!"

No, my dear friend, my attempts so far to scale lofty heights have been unsuccessful. But, even though I am bruised from my falls, I find courage and challenge in knowing that, with God's help, I can dust myself off and try again, remembering always, "At nightfall, weeping enters in, but with the dawn, rejoicing."